Getting Started

with

Middle School

Sentence

Composing

Getting Started
with
Middle School Sentence Composing

A Student Worktext

Don and Jenny Killgallon

HEINEMANN
Portsmouth, NH

Heinemann

145 Maplewood Ave., Suite 300

Portsmouth, NH 03801

www.heinemann.com

Offices and agents throughout the world

Library of Congress Cataloging-in-Publication Data

Names: Killgallon, Don, author. | Killgallon, Jenny, author.

Title: Getting started with middle school sentence composing: a student worktext / Don and Jenny Killgallon.

Description: Portsmouth, NH : Heinemann, [2019] | Audience: Grade 6 to 8.

Identifiers: LCCN 2018051331 | ISBN 9780325107318

Subjects: LCSH: English language—Sentences—Study and teaching (Middle School) | English language—Composition and exercises—Study and teaching (Middle School) | English language—Sentences—Problems, exercises, etc.

Classification: LCC LB1576 .K4819 2019 | DDC 428.0071/2—dc23

LC record available at https://lccn.loc.gov/2018051331

Acquisitions Editor: Tobey Antao

Production Editor: Sean Moreau

Cover Designers: Monica Ann Crigler and Sean Moreau

Interior Designer: Monica Ann Crigler

Typesetter: Valerie Levy, Drawing Board Studios

Manufacturing: Steve Bernier

Printed in the United States of America on acid-free paper

4 5 6 7 RWP 24 23 22 21

August 2021 Printing

CONTENTS

This book uses an original approach to strengthen your sentences by imitating authors at their best. Learning from their way of building sentences can improve your skill as a sentence builder. You will learn how to use their sentence-composing power tools to write more strongly and read more skillfully to be at your best.

QUICKSHOTS FOR NEW WORDS 1

Inside, you'll meet new words, but you'll get instant help to learn what they mean. A quickshot is a familiar word placed right next to an unfamiliar word to keep you reading smoothly.

BASIC TRAINING

Before learning how to build better sentences, you need to know what a sentence is, what its parts are, and what tools good writers use to build strong sentences.

SUBJECTS AND PREDICATES 6

SENTENCE-COMPOSING TOOLS 12

REPAIRING BROKEN SENTENCES

Sentence-composing tools are sentence parts, not complete sentences. If a tool is written with a capital letter and ends with a period, it is a broken sentence, just a piece of a sentence, a fragment. In this section you'll learn to spot and repair broken sentences, or, even better, avoid them in your writing.

FRAGMENTS 21

LEARNING BY IMITATING   29

To learn how to do something, imitate people who know how. In this section, you'll see how to build better sentences by imitating those who really know how. In the next section, you'll use imitation to learn places within a sentence authors use to build their sentences in ways you can build your sentences.

PREVIEW: THE SENTENCE-COMPOSING POSITIONS   40

After this preview of the positions—**openers, splits, closers**—you'll learn and practice each position.

OPENERS: GOOD BEGINNINGS   45

You'll imitate and compose sentences like this:

> **His hand trembling,** Billy laid the peanut-butter-and-fried-worm sandwich down on the table.
>
> —Thomas Rockwell, *How to Eat Fried Worms*

SPLITS: GOOD ADDITIONS   60

You'll imitate and compose sentences like this:

> This leader, **whose word was law among boys who defied authority for the sake of defiance,** was no more than twelve or thirteen years old and looked even younger.
>
> —Henry Gregor Felsen, "Horatio"

CLOSERS: GOOD ENDINGS   76

You'll imitate and compose sentences like this:

> He was a mean-looking man, **red in the face and bearded.**
>
> —Mildred D. Taylor, *Roll of Thunder, Hear My Cry*

REVIEW: THE SENTENCE-COMPOSING POSITIONS   92

> In this review of the positions—**openers, splits, closers**—you'll see how famous authors use those positions.

MIXES: GOOD VARIETY   96

You'll imitate and compose sentences like this:

> **After a minute**, two of the creatures, **a doe and her fawn**, moved hesitantly down the slope, **looking at him curiously**.
>
> —Alexander Key, *The Forgotten Door*

THE TOOLBOX   114

To get the job done right in your sentences, use the right tools in the right places. You've learned all of the right places to build stronger sentences. Those power places are in your toolbox. Get ready to use them in this section. When you finish, admire your work, done right with the right tools in the right places, and take a bow.

THE SENTENCE-COMPOSING APPROACH

Nothing is more satisfying than to write a good sentence.

—Barbara Tuchman, historian

QUICKSHOTS FOR NEW WORDS

Sentences sometimes contain unfamiliar words. Take the opening of this famous speech by President Abraham Lincoln, honoring the memory of soldiers buried at Gettysburg after a huge battle there in the American Civil War.

Four score and seven years ago our fathers brought forth on this continent a new nation, conceived in Liberty, and dedicated to the proposition that all men are created equal.

Now we are engaged in a great civil war, testing whether that nation, or any nation so conceived and dedicated, can long endure. We are met on a great battle-field of that war. We have come to dedicate a portion of that field, as a final resting place for those who here gave their lives that that nation might live. It is altogether fitting and proper that we should do this.

Even the beginning, "four score and seven years ago," isn't easy to figure out. The meaning is roughly this: Something happened in the past. How far in the past? The only way to know for sure is to know what the word *score* means. Maybe it's time for a dictionary dive. Other words in President Lincoln's speech also create hurdles maybe too high to jump over, halting understanding.

Dictionary diving for all those would take time, a long time, preventing smooth reading.

Good news: In this worktext, you don't need a dictionary. Throughout this worktext when individual words are bold, a fast definition—a quickshot

—will be adjacent. If you already know the word, just keep reading. If you don't, a quickshot will keep you reading without stumbling.

Although quickshots may not give you the full meaning of a word, with their help you can skip the dictionary and keep reading. Now reread the opening of Lincoln's Gettysburg Address, this time with quickshots.

---

*Four **score** [twenty] and seven years ago our*
***fathers** [ancestors] brought forth on this continent,*
*a new nation, **conceived** [created] in **liberty***
*[freedom], and **dedicated** [devoted] to the **proposition***
[belief] that all men are created equal.

*Now we are **engaged** [fighting] in a great civil war,*
testing whether that nation, or any nation so conceived
*and dedicated, can long **endure** [survive]. We are **met***
[gathered] on a great battlefield of that war. We have come
*to dedicate a **portion** [section] of that field, as a **final***
***resting place** [cemetery] for those who here gave their*
*lives that that nation might live. It is altogether **fitting***

*[right] and **proper** [appropriate] that we should do this.*

As you now know, the word *score* means twenty years, and the word *seven* means, well, seven, so "four score and seven years ago" means eighty-seven years earlier. Lincoln was speaking in 1863. When you do the math (1863 minus 87) you get 1776, the year of the birthday of our country.

QUICKSHOTS IN THIS WORKTEXT

If a word might be a problem, there's a quickshot to help you keep reading. The quickshot unlocks the word's meaning. Knowing the word's meaning often also unlocks the meaning of the sentence.

Here is another example of quickshots. Following is a description of Pickwick meeting a group of children for the first time. You'll see the description first without quickshots, and then with quickshots.

DESCRIPTION WITHOUT QUICKSHOTS

(1) We who loved Pickwick used to forget what a **shock** to a stranger the first **sight** of him was. (2) He sank his **ponderous bulk** down into a chair and **requested** coffee. (3) He loved children as much as Father did, but while children took to Father immediately, Pickwick had to **win them over**. (4) I brought him his coffee and watched him look around in **mock consternation**. (5) "But there's no table to set it on," he **cried, glancing** around to make sure the children were watching. (6) "Well, luckily I brought my own!" (7) And **with that**, he set his cup and saucer on his own **protruding paunch**. (8) I never knew a child who could **resist** this trick. (9) Soon a **respectful circle** of children gathered round him.

—Corrie ten Boom, *The Hiding Place* (adapted)

DESCRIPTION WITH QUICKSHOTS

(1) We who loved Pickwick used to forget what a **shock** [*surprise*] to a stranger the first **sight** [*appearance*] of him was. (2) He sank his **ponderous** [*heavy*] **bulk** [*size*] down into a chair and **requested** [*asked for*] coffee. (3) He loved children as much as Father did, but while children took to Father immediately, Pickwick had to **win them over** [*convince them*]. (4) I brought him his coffee and watched him look

around in **mock** [*pretend*] **consternation** [*surprise*]. (5) "But there's no table to set it on," he **cried** [*shouted*], **glancing** [*looking*] around to make sure the children were watching. (6) "Well, luckily I brought my own!" (7) And **with that** [*then*] he set his cup and saucer on his own **protruding** [*sticking out*] **paunch** [*stomach*]. (8) I never knew a child who could **resist** [*hold out against*] this trick. (9) Soon a **respectful circle** [*audience*] of children gathered round him.

DESCRIPTION WITH JUST THE EASIER WORDS

(1) We who loved Pickwick used to forget what a shock to a stranger the first appearance of him was. (2) He sank his heavy size down into a chair and asked for coffee. (3) He loved children as much as Father did, but while children took to Father immediately, Pickwick had to convince them. (4) I brought him his coffee and watched him look around in pretend surprise. (5) "But there's no table to set it on," he shouted, looking around to make sure the children were watching. (6) "Well, luckily I brought my own!" (7) And then he set his cup and saucer on his own sticking-out stomach. (8) I never knew a child who could **resist** this trick. (9) Soon a respectful audience of children gathered round him.

I ran across many words whose meanings I did not know, and I either looked them up in a dictionary or, before I had a chance to do that, **encountered** [*met*] *the word in a* **context** [*sentence*] *that made its meaning clear.*

—Richard Wright, *Black Boy*

With quickshots, you don't need to look up new words, or struggle to figure them out.

QUIZ: QUICKSHOTS

Directions: Quickshots are very short, so they are easier than dictionary definitions to remember. See how many you remember. Match the word with its definition.

1. **Liberty** is a value that the United States of America approves and supports.

   a. freedom   **b.** honesty   **c.** dignity   **d.** morality

2. When a person is **dedicated to** a sport, he or she will practice hard to improve.

   a. interested in   **b.** enthralled by   **c.** devoted to   **d.** fascinated by

3. After the tailor measured it, Samuel was surprised to learn the size of his **paunch**.

   a. arm   **b.** shoulder   **c.** muscle   **d.** stomach

4. My dad was **glancing** around the auto showroom with great curiosity and interest.

   a. starting   **b.** looking   **c.** walking   **d.** strolling

5. Before the big test, I reread the most important **portion** of the novel because I knew there would be questions about it.

   a. chapter   **b.** scene   **c.** page   **d.** section

6. The principal insisted that students wear **proper** clothes to the banquet honoring our championship basketball team.

   a. formal   **b.** colorful   **c.** appropriate   **d.** pretty

7. When the new students arrived in class, Mrs. Santina knew she was going to have to **win them over**.

   a. like them   **b.** ignore them   **c.** convince them   **d.** overlook them

8. Sometimes to learn about our legal system in history class, we participate in **mock** trials.

   a. pretend   **b.** illegal   **c.** historic   **d.** amusing

BASIC TRAINING

SUBJECTS AND PREDICATES

A sentence is a comment about a topic. The topic is called *a subject*. The comment about the topic is called *a predicate*. Every sentence needs both a subject and a predicate. Look at these sentences about an unusual African animal named an aardvark. Even the spelling of its name is unusual because it begins with two *a*'s.

Subject (topic)	Predicate (comment about the topic)
1. All aardvarks	have large piglike noses that they use to sniff out termites for food.
2. They	use their powerful claws and legs to dig deep into termite and ant holes to capture those insects during the night.
3. An aardvark's sharp claws	dig holes in search of underground ants.
4. Evidence of the existence of aardvarks	appeared in prehistoric times.
5. An aardvark's diet	consists mainly of ants and termites.

ACTIVITY 1: MATCHING SUBJECTS AND PREDICATES

Directions: Match the subject with its predicate to make a sentence. Write out each sentence.

Subjects	Predicates
1. Hot soup ^ —Kelly Yang, *Front Desk*	**a.** is a mix of tourists who've wandered too far from Times Square and actual working New Yorkers wishing the tourists would just go back to Times Square.
2. The sun ^ —Aisha Saeed, *Amal Unbound*	**b. swarmed** [*gathered*] about my family, guiding them into the church.
3. Deacons and church ladies in white dresses ^ —Jewell Parker Rhodes, *Ghost Boys* (adapted)	**c.** splashed onto customers.
4. The crowd ^ —Nicola Yoon, *The Sun Is Also a Star*	**d.** gonged as he spat the gum inside.

5. The metal trash can ^
   —David Barclay Moore,
   The Stars Beneath Our Feet
	e. blazed **overhead** [*above*], warming my **chador** [*scarf*] and my hair beneath it.

- -

ACTIVITY 2: CREATING SUBJECTS

Directions: Write interesting subjects for these predicates to make a complete sentence. Make your subjects several words long as in the following example.

EXAMPLE

     Predicate: . . . hoped that the storm would blow way out into the desert that stretched before them like an ocean.

POSSIBLE SUBJECTS (Topics):

a. The members of the group hoped that the storm would blow way out into the desert that stretched before them like an ocean.

b. The terrified townspeople hoped that the storm would blow way out into the desert that stretched before them like an ocean.

c. People with friends in the affected area hoped that the storm would blow way out into the desert that stretched before them like an ocean.

Author's Sentence:

The ten-year-old girl Lucky hoped strongly that the storm would blow way out into the desert that stretched before them like an ocean.

—Susan Patron, *The Higher Power of Lucky*

---

1. . . . was curled up on the brown velvet armchair, which years ago he'd staked out as his own.

—Deborah and James Howe, *Bunnicula: A Rabbit-Tale of Mystery*

2. . . . sped through the intersection against the red light and roared directly toward the Hardys and Chet.

—Franklin W. Dixon, *The Secret of the Old Mill*

3. . . . was an elegant young man, **tautly** [*tightly*] muscled, with a shock of orange hair.

—Laura Hillenbrand, *Seabiscuit*

4. . . . **hoisted** [*lifted*] a toddler onto her shoulder.

—Barbara Kingsolver, *Animal Dreams*

5. . . . saw the head of an animal, motionless, partially hidden in the **fronds** [*ferns*] with the two large dark eyes watching him coldly.

—Michael Crichton, *Jurassic Park*

ACTIVITY 3: CREATING PREDICATES

Directions: Write interesting predicates for these subjects to make complete sentences. Make your predicates several words long as in the following example.

EXAMPLE

Subject: A cobra . . .

SAMPLE PREDICATES:

a. A cobra **slithered slowly through the grass near the deep jungle.**

b. A cobra **showed its readiness to strike by spreading its hood wide.**

c. A cobra **is a very dangerous reptile that you should not go near.**

Author's Sentence:
A cobra was coiled in the mud barely six feet away from her, its hood spread wide, swaying in the yellow light.

—Lauren St. John, *The White Giraffe*

1. The pig behind the stove . . .
    —Bill and Vera Cleaver, *Where the Lilies Bloom* (adapted)

2. Every inch of my skin . . .
    —Carrie Ryan, *The Forest of Hands and Teeth*

3. Police car doors . . .

> —Robert Lipsyte, *The Contender*

4. An old barn with red paint turning dark purple . . .

> —Keith Donohue, *The Stolen Child*

5. The Jeep far below him . . .

> —Robb White, *Deathwatch* (adapted)

QUIZ: SUBJECTS AND PREDICATES

Directions: Jot down whether the statement is true or false.

1. Sometimes complete sentences contain only a subject (topic) but no predicate (comment about that topic).

2. Sometimes complete sentences contain only a predicate but no subject.

3. The following sentence contains a subject with two parts, not one.

    Smoke and flames were pouring out of the blackened spaces where the windows had been.

    > —Franklin W. Dixon, *The Secret of the Old Mill*

4. The following sentence contains a predicate with exactly three parts.

    Miss Honey paused and leaned back in her chair behind the plain table.

    > —Roald Dahl, *Matilda* (adapted)

5. All complete sentences contain both a subject, which is a topic, and a predicate, which is a comment about the topic.

MY WRITING: INFORMATIONAL SENTENCES

Pretend you are writing a brochure about insects. Online or offline, find out lots of interesting information about one of these fascinating insects: wasps, spiders, ticks, scorpions, tarantulas, mosquitoes, termites, gnats, bumblebees, centipedes, fleas—or some other insect.

Then write five sentences between ten and twenty words long about your insect. Make sure each sentence has an informative subject (topic) and predicate (comment about the subject).

BASIC TRAINING

SENTENCE-COMPOSING TOOLS

What makes the best pizza? First, you'll need two basics: crust and filling. Then you'll want more: maybe cheese, meat sauce, onions, peppers, pepperoni, or the works. Add-ons make it tastier, and the best.

What makes the best sentence? First, you'll need two requirements: a subject and a predicate. Although those two parts are necessary, they are not the most important sentence parts of best sentences.

The most important parts are sentence-composing tools. They add detail to your sentences, providing information beyond the subject and predicate. Like pizza, add-ons also make sentences tastier, and the best.

Take a look at the following examples. The first sentence in each pair has just a subject and predicate. The second sentence has the same subject and predicate but also sentence-composing tools. Tools are bolded.

On the Mark: Tools need commas to separate them from the rest of the sentence.

EXAMPLES

1a. Mr. Murry rose.

1b. Mr. Murry, **who had been sitting, his elbows on his knees, his chin on his fists,** rose.
> —Madeleine L'Engle, *A Wrinkle in Time*

2a. People moved away from him.

2b. **On the platform,** people moved away from him, **wrinkling their noses**.

> —Robert Lipsyte, *The Contender*

3a. She could see a huge slab of ice.

3b. Outside the window, in the blue moonlight, she could see a huge slab of ice, **sticking up from the snow.**

> —Susan Fromberg Schaeffer, *Time in Its Flight*

4a. He could swear that he saw dozens and dozens of flickering ghosts.

4b. He could swear, **as he drove down the tree-lined street in the late morning light,** that he saw dozens and dozens of flickering ghosts, **watching him, smiling.**

> —Sandhya Menon, *When Dimple Met Rishi*

5a. He had two illnesses.

5b. When he was three, he had two illnesses, **one following the other, terrible high-fevered illnesses, which had almost taken his life and had damaged his brain.**

> —Betsy Byars, *The Summer of the Swans*

ACTIVITY 1: IDENTIFYING SENTENCE PARTS

Directions: Jot down the letter for the kind of sentence part:

S for subject

P for predicate

T for tool

Note: There is a subject (S) and a predicate (P) in each list. The other sentence parts are tools (T).

EXAMPLE *(Commas separate tools from the rest of the sentence.)*

a. In a panic,

b. I

c. punched the nose of the huge shark.

—Willard Price, *Diving Adventure*

ANSWERS

a: T

b: S

c: P

PART ONE

These sentences contain a subject and a predicate and just one tool.

1a. Jody

1b. continued on through the large vegetable patch,

1c. where the green corn was higher than his head.

—John Steinbeck, *The Red Pony*

2a. Unsteadily,

2b. she

2c. limped [*walked awkwardly*] across the room.

—Eleanor Coerr, *Sadako and the Thousand Paper Cranes*

3a. As the dragon charged,

3b. it

3c. released huge clouds of hissing steam through its nostrils.

—Heywood Broun, *The Fifty-First Dragon*

4a. The children,

4b. shouting,

4c. came charging back into their homeroom.

—Rosa Guy, *The Friends*

5a. The most dangerous shark

5b. is the one that is both hungry and mean,

5c. like the powerful mako that lives near the island of Bora Bora in the Pacific Ocean.

—Willard Price, *Diving Adventure*

PART TWO

These sentences contain a subject, a predicate, and more than one tool.

6a. Slowly,

6b. noiselessly,

6c. I

6d. turned myself in that direction.

—Suzanne Collins, *The Hunger Games*

7a. Something

7b. dashed [*ran*] across the road,

7c. a white flash in his headlights,

7d. like a large rat.

—Michael Crichton, *Jurassic Park*

8a. In her soft voice,

8b. which still held a **slight** [*small*] **trace** [*amount*] of her Texas accent,

8c. she

8d. read him nursery rhymes and fairy tales and hundreds of picture books,

8e. taken home every Saturday from the library.

—Katherine Paterson, Park's Quest

9a. Year after year,

9b. learning to be quiet,

9c. Michael K.

9d. sat on a blanket,

9e. watching his mother polish other people's floors.

—J. M. Coetzee, Life and Times of Michael K

10a. In an instant,

10b. in the blink of an eye,

10c. we

10d. crossed over from this wasteland into a place carpeted with green grass,

10e. with trees along both sides of the road and flower beds running down the middle of a median strip.

—Edward Bloor, Tangerine

QUESTIONS: What two sentence parts cannot be removed without destroying the sentence? What sentence parts can be removed without destroying the sentence, but good writers don't remove them because they add information and tastiness to sentences?

SENTENCE-COMPOSING TOOL FACTS

A tool is a sentence part that adds detail to a sentence.

1. Tools can be placed in the *beginning*, *middle*, or *end* of a sentence.	They can appear in the beginning, with a *comma after the tool*. **When an aardvark is preparing for its family**, it digs into the earth to create a safe place for the young. They can appear in the middle with a *comma before and after the tool*. An aardvark's thick skin, **its protection against enemies**, can save an aardvark from clawed and poisonous animals. They can appear at the end with a *comma before the tool*. Aardvarks use their keen hearing to detect enemies, **including lions, leopards, cheetahs, hyenas, and pythons**.
2. A tool can be a *word*.	**Surprisingly**, the cucumber is the only fruit eaten by an aardvark, which prefers ants and termites.
3. A tool can be a *phrase*. A phrase is a group of words without a subject and predicate.	Aardvarks, **running in zigzags from an enemy**, can avoid being attacked.
4. A tool can be a *dependent clause*. A dependent clause is a sentence part containing a subject and predicate, but it is not a sentence, only a part of a sentence.	**Since an aardvark is nocturnal**, it only comes out at night.

5. Sentences can have several tools, together or apart.	Tools Together **Looking for food, their ears pointing forward indicating both smell and hearing are involved,** they zigzag as they search. Tools Apart **With its long sticky tongue,** an aardvark can take up each night as many as fifty thousand insects to eat, **not stopping until it eats all of them.**
6. Tools can be short, medium, or long.	Short **In the early night,** they are the most active in seeking food. Medium Aardvarks, **if weather is rainy or windy,** stay in their underground homes. Long **Pausing at the entrance to its burrow to sniff and determine the presence or absence of enemies,** an aardvark will wait about ten minutes.

QUIZ: SENTENCE-COMPOSING TOOLS

Directions: Jot down whether the statement is true or false.

1. Tools are complete sentences.

2. Tools can be placed at the beginning or end of a sentence but not in the middle of a sentence.

3. This sentence contains exactly one tool:

   It was like two invisible puppeteers, standing stage left and right, were yanking on strings to lift up the corners of her mouth.

   —Sandhya Menon, *When Dimple Met Rishi*

4. The following sentence contains a subject and a predicate but no tools:

   At the foot of one of the trees, the boy's father sat, with the lantern still burning by his side.

   —William Armstrong, *Sounder*

5. In the following sentence, the sentence part with the fewest words is the subject:

   As they stepped out the back door, Mama looked back at us, her eyes uncertain, as if she did not want to leave us.

   —Mildred D. Taylor, *Roll of Thunder, Hear My Cry*

MY WRITING: INFORMATIONAL SENTENCES

Find out more information about some other insect. Then write five sentences between ten and twenty words long about your insect. In each sentence, be sure to include a subject and predicate and one or more sentence-composing tools.

REVIEW:

- For **subjects and predicates,** reread the sentences about aardvarks on page 6.

- For **sentence-composing tools,** reread the sentences about aardvarks on pages 17–18.

REPAIRING BROKEN SENTENCES

FRAGMENTS

A fragment looks like a sentence because it has a capital letter at the beginning and a period at the end, but it is not a sentence. It is a broken sentence, only a sentence part, just a fragment of a complete sentence.

EXAMPLES

1a. *Fragment*—At one thirty in the morning.

1b. *Sentence*—At one thirty in the morning, my eyes are burning and my stomach cries from hunger.

> —Ibi Zoboi, *American Street*

2a. *Fragment*—Who even as an infant had seldom cried.

2b. *Sentence*—Charles Wallace, who even as an infant had **seldom** [*rarely*] cried, was near tears.

> —Madeleine L'Engle, *A Wrinkle in Time*

3a. *Fragment*—Getting his mouth washed out with soap.

3b. *Sentence* —Charles said the bad word himself three or four times, getting his mouth washed out with soap.

> —Shirley Jackson, *"Charles"*

4a. *Fragment*—Moving his arm only a little.

4b. *Sentence*—Moving his arm only a little, he stared in amazement at a small, purplish hole in it halfway between his wrist and his elbow.

> —Robb White, *Deathwatch*

5a. *Fragment*—Carrying his **severed** [*cut off*] leg.

5b. *Sentence* —Muldoon was walking back toward the Jeep, carrying his severed leg.

—Michael Crichton, Jurassic Park

Plates accidentally broken into fragments can be repaired, and so can sentences broken into fragments. In this section, you will learn how to fix broken sentences, or—even better—avoid them completely.

ACTIVITY 1: SPOTTING AND GLUING FRAGMENTS

Directions: Each group has a sentence and two fragments. Tell which is the sentence and which are the two fragments. Then glue the fragments back into the sentence at the beginning or the end—whichever makes more sense.

On the Mark: When you glue fragments into sentences, commas are needed.

EXAMPLE

a. Fearing that the librarian would call me back for further questioning. (*fragment*)

b. I went out of the library. (*sentence*)

c. Not daring to glance at the books. (*fragment*)

Good Arrangements:

Not daring to glance at the books, fearing that the librarian would call me back for further questioning, I went out of the library. (*Both are glued at the beginning of the sentence.*)

OR

> Not daring to glance at the books, I went out of the library, <u>fearing</u> <u>that the librarian would call me back for further questioning.</u> (*One is glued at the beginning of the sentence, and one at the end of the sentence.*)
>
> —Richard Wright, *Black Boy*

1a. In the predawn darkness.

1b. Listening.

1c. A twelve-year-old-boy sat up in bed.

> —Laura Hillenbrand, *Unbroken*

2a. If Harlem was a human body.

2b. 125th Street would be its pumping heart.

2c. Throbbing all the time.

> —David Barclay Moore, *The Stars Beneath Our Feet*

3a. Shielding the lenses of their flashlights.

3b. The boys began a thorough search of the wooded section.

3c. So that the light beams would not be easily **detected** [*seen*] by anyone **lurking** [*hiding*] in the **vicinity** [*area*].

> —Franklin W. Dixon, *The Secret of the Old Mill*

4a. Hurling them into the air like confetti.

4b. Children love to play in piles of leaves.

4c. Leaping into soft unruly mattresses of them.

> —Diane Ackerman, *A Natural History of the Senses*

5a. He saw a movement on the ground and heard a scraping sound.

5b. Watching a rat take its head out of a paper bag and regard him.

5c. As he walked toward the freight house.

—John Cheever, "The Five-Forty-Eight"

ACTIVITY 2: GLUING BROKEN SENTENCES BACK TOGETHER

Directions: The following paragraph has *five* fragments that make reading bumpy. Glue each fragment to the sentence where it belongs—the sentence before the fragment, or the sentence following the fragment, whichever makes more sense. When you finish, you will have *three* complete sentences and no fragments. Then, reading will be smooth, not bumpy.

On the Mark: When you glue fragments into sentences, often commas are needed.

Halloween Memories

(1) When kids went out on that special fall night of Halloween. (2) Carrying empty bags they hoped to bring back filled with candy. (3) Their costumes always reflected the current **craze** [*popular trend*]. (4) A while ago, it seemed that every second boy who showed up at my door was wearing Harry Potter eyeglasses. (5) And a lightning-bolt-scar **decal** [*design*] on his forehead. (6) On my own **maiden** [*first*] voyage as a candy-beggar, many **moons** [*years*] ago. (7) I went walking down the sidewalk with my mother trailing ten feet behind me. (8) Wearing a stormtrooper costume from a *Star Wars* movie.

—Stephen King, 11/22/63

ACTIVITY 3: SOLVING A FRAGMENT PUZZLE

Directions: The following paragraph, about an injury from a fall down a steep path, has to be put back together. Underneath the paragraph are five broken sentences (fragments) that are parts of sentences in the original paragraph. While copying the paragraph, glue each fragment to the sentence where it belongs. <u>Hint</u>: The fragments are listed after the paragraph in the order they occur in the original paragraph.

On the Mark: When you glue a fragment into a sentence, use a comma.

The Fall

(1) He ran blindly down the mountain path. (2) Several times he fell, but was on his feet again in the next breath. (3) He fell hard onto his face. (4) He spat blood.

—Linda Sue Park, *A Single Shard* (adapted)

FRAGMENTS

Note: A capitalized fragment begins a sentence in the paragraph. Other fragments end a sentence in the paragraph.

a. Heedless [*unaware*] of the rocks and shrubs

b. stumbling, tripping, skidding in a head-first **descent** [*downward fall*].

c. When at last he reached the point where the path leveled out

d. the dirt mixing with his tears

e. His teeth cutting into his top lip

ACTIVITY 4: REPAIRING BROKEN SENTENCES

Directions: Make the fragment a part of a complete sentence.

EXAMPLE

Fragment: because the snowstorm closed school

SAMPLE REPAIRS:

a. Because the snowstorm closed school, I had some extra time to complete the homework I forgot to do.

b. The basketball game against Westport High School's team was canceled because the snowstorm closed school.

Directions for 1–5: Make the fragment into a sentence part at the beginning of a complete sentence.

1. *Fragment*: When the pizza was delivered to our apartment.

   Sample Repair: When the pizza was delivered to our apartment, we started eating it immediately.

2. *Fragment*: To learn how to save money.

   Sample Repair: To learn how to save money, you should put away some of your earnings.

3. *Fragment*: Late that night when I got home from work.

   Sample Repair: Late that night when I got home from work, I learned that a good friend had been in an automobile accident.

4. *Fragment*: Telling her friends what her native country was like.

   Sample Repair: Telling her friends what her native country was like, Luciana felt her nervousness melt away.

5. *Fragment*: Staying up too late playing games or watching movies.

   Sample Repair: Staying up too late playing games or watching movies, I am not very alert in my classes.

Directions for 6–10: Make the fragment into a sentence part *at the end* of a complete sentence.

6. *Fragment*: One of the most enjoyable experiences I've ever had.

   Sample Repair: White water rafting down the Shenandoah River is one of the most enjoyable experiences I've ever had.

7. *Fragment*: Causing a broken arm that took a long time to heal.

   Sample Repair: My little sister Alicia fell off the fence, causing a broken arm that took a long time to heal.

8. *Fragment*: Which my boss always emphasizes as important to all new employees.

   Sample Repair: Being on time matters, which my boss always emphasizes as important to all new employees.

9. *Fragment*: My brother who sometimes hides in the basement.

   Sample Repair: The whole family was enlisted to help find Fred, my brother who sometimes hides in the basement

10. *Fragment*: Running faster to keep up with the rest of the team.

    Sample Repair: Anita kept going even though she was exhausted, running faster to keep up with the rest of the team.

QUIZ: FRAGMENTS

Directions: Jot down whether the statement is true or false.

1. Fragments are always sentence parts instead of complete sentences.

2. Fragments cannot be repaired.

3. Putting a capital letter at the beginning of a fragment and a period at its end sometimes repairs a fragment.

4. Fragments can always be joined to the sentence that comes before them, but never to the sentence that comes after them.

5. The following paragraph contains exactly three fragments.

> Wide awake now, he pushed back the covers, got out of bed, and went over to the window. In the pale half-light of the moon. He could clearly see the church tower up on the small hill behind his house. The one with the train tracks curving beside it. The moon shone on the graveyard attached to the church. Filled with tombstones you could hardly read anymore. He could also see the great yew tree that rose from the center of the graveyard. A tree so ancient it almost seemed to be made of the same stone as the church.

> —Patrick Ness, *A Monster Calls* (adapted)

LEARNING BY IMITATING

"Show me how to do it." You've probably asked somebody to show you how to do something: swing a bat, style your hair, ride a bike, make a grilled cheese sandwich, solve a math problem—how to do just about anything.

Those activities, and many more, show that imitating is a good way to learn. Throughout this worktext, you'll see how authors build their sentences, imitate how they do it, and then build your sentences as they do.

First, look at some sentence imitations. Below is a model followed by five imitations of that model. All six sentences—the model and the imitations—mean something different, but they all have the same kinds of sentence parts. In other words, the imitations are built like the model.

MODEL SENTENCE:

Backing from under the porch on his hands and knees, he touched the lantern and tipped it over.

—William H. Armstrong, *Sounder*

IMITATION SENTENCES:

1. Feeling around with his fingers and hands, the blind man recognized the visitor and greeted him pleasantly.

2. Listening quietly with her mind and heart, the young student understood its importance and treated it seriously.

3. Thinking about the leak with his experience and knowledge, the emergency plumber identified the problem and fixed it easily.

4. Moving toward the sound from the doorbell and intercom, the little girl opened the door and walked through it confidently.

5. Singing into the microphone for the audience and judges, the contestant amazed the audience and finished the song triumphantly.

WHAT MAKES A GOOD MODEL SENTENCE?

Sentences worth imitating appear in almost everything we read. Throughout this worktext are hundreds of model sentences from all kinds of writing, from classics like *To Kill a Mockingbird*, from fantasies like the Harry Potter novels, from popular favorites like *The Hunger Games*, from children's literature like *A Wrinkle in Time*, and from spy stories, horror stories, true stories, love stories, sports stories, funny stories, sci-fi stories, and on and on.

Despite the wide range of sources—from children's literature to classic novels—all the model sentences in *Getting Started with Middle School Sentence Composing* illustrate the use of powerful tools to build strong sentences.

The positions where tools can be used within a sentence—the beginning (opener), middle (split), ending (closer)—are the focus of this worktext. After learning them through the activities in this worktext, you can be a builder of strong sentences. Here are a few examples.

1. From *To Kill a Mockingbird:* **When he was nearly thirteen**, my brother Jem got his arm badly broken at the elbow.

    —Harper Lee

2. From *The Underground:* Earth, **our little blue and green planet, the one with the fluffy white clouds and all**, is under attack.

    —K. A. Applegate

3. From *A Wrinkle in Time:* Charles Wallace slid down from his chair and trotted over to the refrigerator, **his pajamaed feet padding softly as a kitten's**.

    —Madeleine L'Engle

Those three sentences are examples of sentence-building tools you'll learn, practice, and use through the activities in this worktext, then use to build your own strong sentences in and beyond middle school.

ACTIVITY 1: UNDERSTANDING SENTENCE PARTS

Directions: To imitate a sentence, first you need to see its parts. In reading and writing, understanding sentence parts is helpful. Read the following sentences broken into meaningful sentence parts. Pause after each slash mark.

EXAMPLES

1. People are edging closer, / snapping pictures, / taking video / with their phones.

   —Jewell Parker Rhodes, *Ghost Boys*

2. My schoolmates / watched time crawl / every afternoon, / waiting an eternity / for the three o'clock bell.

   —Keith Donohue, *The Stolen Child*

3. Nancy had been dreaming all night, / and when she woke in the morning / it was with the strange sensation / that she had come back / from a long journey, / leaving part of herself behind.

   —Lois Duncan, *A Gift of Magic*

4. I picture myself / at the top of the Eiffel Tower, / climbing pyramids in Egypt, / dancing in the streets in Spain, / riding in a boat in Venice, / and walking on the Great Wall of China.

   —Erika L. Sánchez, *I Am Not Your Perfect Mexican Daughter*

5. John, / who is an older man, / falls in love with Mary, / and Mary, / who is only twenty-two, / feels sorry for him / because he's worried / about his hair falling out.

   —Margaret Atwood, "Happy Endings"

ACTIVITY 2: SPOTTING IMITATION SENTENCES

Directions: Underneath the author's sentence are three sentences. Which *two* sentences imitate the author's sentence because, although different in meaning, they have similar sentence parts?

1. *Model Sentence:* A small man, he wore a cotton shirt and a long, bloodstained smock.

     —Christopher Paolini, *Eragon*

     a. The fastest hunters, cheetahs have a flexible spine and four hard, rubbery feet.

     b. The shopkeeper was not prepared for a group of teenage girls who wanted lipsticks.

     c. A good friend, Janelle told an interesting story and a hilarious, clever joke.

2. *Model Sentence:* After a minute, two of the creatures, a doe and her fawn, moved hesitantly down the **slope** [*hill*] and stood looking at him curiously.

     —Alexander Key, *The Forgotten Door*

     a. After the sunset, all of the tourists, some kids and their parents, walked slowly toward the parking lot and strolled looking for their cars carefully.

     b. In an hour, two of the eggs, a bird and its sibling, hatched noisily in the nest and started peering at the world curiously.

     c. A husband and his wife looked enthusiastically at the house for sale and started talking to each other about whether to buy it.

3. *Model Sentence:* He walked right into the punch, a ton of concrete that slammed into his mouth.

     —Robert Lipsyte, *The Contender*

a. Cinderella danced gracefully to the music, a melody of beauty that contrasted with her life.

b. Alfie slept soundly throughout the night, a time of rest that settled down his nerves.

c. Not sure what would happen next, the security guard watched constantly and intensely.

4. *Model Sentence:* He brushed two saddle horses in the stalls, talking quietly to them all the time.

        —John Steinbeck, *The Red Pony*

a. She petted both little kittens in the box, whispering softly to them all the while.

b. After the rain stopped, she gathered the plants from the porch and took them inside.

c. Mr. Cromwell noticed several small children on the beach, playing happily with each other all the time.

5. *Model Sentence:* I kept my eyes on my hands on the desk, waiting for something to happen, an explosion, a battle cry, a noise, anything but the silence.

        —Rosa Guy, *The Friends*

a. The basketball team approached the court with no confidence at all because they expected not to beat the first-place team.

b. The general led his soldiers into the battle on the field, searching for anything to happen, a shot, a canon roar, a surrender, anything but a defeat.

c. The scientist kept his attention on the test tubes in the rack, hoping for many changes to occur, a combination, a different color, a reaction, everything but a disappointment.

ACTIVITY 3: MATCHING MODEL AND IMITATION SENTENCES

Directions: Match the imitation with the model it imitates.

Model Sentence	Imitation Sentence
1. Stepping upon the cold surface, Buck's feet sank into a white mushy something that felt like mud. —Jack London, *The Call of the Wild* (adapted)	**a.** Leaping with power, the dolphin broke the water's surface, feeling it open from the power of its jump.
2. Shivering with nausea, Regis pulled the leech away, feeling it tear from the flesh of his lips. —Michael Crichton, *Jurassic Park*	**b.** Whispering a prayer under her breath so that her family and friends would be safe, she began to smile.
3. Wanda Gambling, a well-known movie star on her way to 96th Street, once got stuck behind a gasoline truck. —Jean Merrill, *The Pushcart War* (adapted)	**c.** Hail and lightning, scattering the audience in minutes, arose suddenly to end the outdoor rock concert.
4. Stacey and T.J., ignoring the rest of us, wandered off to be with the other seventh grade boys. —Mildred D. Taylor, *Roll of Thunder, Hear My Cry*	**d.** Looking into the dark heavens, the astronomer noticed in a starry sky a constellation that looked like dots.
5. Holding a hand before her eyes so that other patients and visitors could not see, she began to weep. —J. M. Coetzee, *Life and Times of Michael K*	**e.** The mosquito, a bothersome local insect on the lookout for fresh blood, sometimes gets swatted by an irritated host.

ACTIVITY 4: UNSCRAMBLING TO IMITATE

Directions: Unscramble the sentence parts to imitate the model sentence. Start with the first sentence part listed.

On the Mark: Put commas where they appear in the model.

EXAMPLE

> *Model Sentence:* Her heart hammering in her chest, Clary ducked behind the nearest concrete pillar and looked around it.
>
> —Cassandra Clare, *City of Bones*

SENTENCE PARTS TO UNSCRAMBLE TO IMITATE THE MODEL SENTENCE:

a. (*Start here.*) His blood gushing from the wound

b. and screamed for help

c. Sammy

d. raced toward the crowded parking lot

Imitation Sentence: <u>His blood gushing from the wound</u>, Sammy raced toward the crowded parking lot and screamed for help.

1. *Model Sentence:* All four members of Maxwell, the other team in the final round, were in the eighth grade.
   —E. L. Konigsburg, *The View from Saturday*

   a. (*Start here.*) All ten cheerleaders

   b. were with their team coach

   c. at Avery

   d. the best squad in the final competition

2. *Model Sentence:* Artemis **generally** [*usually*] had this effect on people, an adolescent speaking with the authority and vocabulary of a powerful adult.

—Eoin Colfer, *Artemis Fowl*

   a. (*Start here.*) Mandela

   b. with the hope and inspiration of a blossoming leader

   c. often created great enthusiasm in people

   d. a survivor sparkling

3. *Model Sentence:* He lifted the **stump** [*remainder*] of the severed leg out of the **foliage** [*bushes*], raising it into the light of the headlamps as blood from the stump gushed down over his hand.

—Michael Crichton, *Jurassic Park*

   a. (*Start here.*) He

   b. as notes from the orchestra sounded loudly over the theater

   c. pounding it with the strength of his arms

   d. hit the gong of the loudest drum in the orchestra

4. *Model Sentence:* After the first weeks of school, when everything seemed gloomy and I still worried a great deal about having left home, things started to get easier.

—Ved Mehta, "A Donkey in a World of Horses" (adapted)

   a. (*Start here.*) After the sudden attack on 9-11

   b. at the twin towers of the World Trade Center

   c. when confusion was constant

   d. shock started to set in

   e. and the nation barely processed the terrifying attack

5. *Model Sentence:* He **scrutinized** [*looked at*] the beggars at the door, a woman with a bent back, an old blind man praying, and many other **wretched** [*unfortunate*] **alms-seekers** [*beggars*].

—Eric P. Kelly, *The Trumpeter of Krakow* (adapted)

a. (*Start here.*) Jason

b. and several more community members

c. a mother with a small child

d. a senior citizen reading

e. registered the voters in the gym

ACTIVITY 5: IMITATING MODEL SENTENCES

Directions: Study the model sentence and a sample imitation to see how both sentences are built alike. Then write your own imitation about something you know, something you've experienced, or something you've seen in media.

Tip: Take it easy. Imitate one sentence part at a time because the best way to eat an elephant is one bite at a time. Here are the sentence parts of the model and its imitation parts.

Model Sentence Parts	Imitation Sentence Parts
1. a. Little Man,	**a.** Hurricane Irma,
b. a very small six-year-old	**b.** a very big fast-moving storm
c. and a most **finicky** [*fussy*] dresser,	**c.** and a powerful wind maker,
d. was brushing his hair	**d.** was coming ashore
e. when I entered.	**e.** when we vacationed.
—Mildred D. Taylor, *Song of the Trees*	

Model Sentence Parts	Imitation Sentence Parts
2. a. Fussing with her skirt, **b.** straightening it, **c.** she looked across the room **d.** to Romey and Ima Dean. —Bill and Vera Cleaver, *Where the Lilies Bloom*	**a.** Dangling over the falls, **b.** watching them, **c.** the daredevil looked into the crowd **d.** for his wife and kids.
3. a. As the gong of the bell sounded **b.** across the playground, **c.** I picked up my pencils **d.** and notebook **e.** and ran inside. —Mildred D. Taylor, *Roll of Thunder, Hear My Cry*	**a.** After the signs of the dawn appeared **b.** in her window, **c.** Glenda turned over her blanket **d.** and sheets **e.** and got up.
4. a. Its engine snarling **b.** like a hunting panther, **c.** the car jolted forward **d.** so fast that my body slammed **e.** into the black leather seat, **f.** my stomach flattening against my spine. —Stephenie Meyer, *Breaking Dawn*	**a.** Its approach nearing **b.** like a terrifying monster, **c.** the tiger moved nearby **d.** so close that my heart pounded **e.** under my heavy breathing chest, **f.** my fear rising with each second.

Learning to build strong sentences by imitating the way authors build strong sentences makes sense because it works.

In the next section, you'll see three sentence-composing places within a sentence authors use to build their strong sentences: beginning, middle, and end. Then, in the rest of this worktext, you'll learn, practice, and use those places to build your sentences the way authors build theirs.

QUIZ: LEARNING BY IMITATING

Directions: Jot down whether the statement is true or false.

1. Imitating is a common way to learn something.

2. Imitating sentences by authors means using most of their words in your own sentence structure.

3. Imitating sentences by authors means using their sentence structure but your own words.

4. Imitating how an author's model sentence is built requires building your sentence mostly like the author's sentence.

5. All three sentences underneath the model sentence imitate how that model is built.

   Model Sentence: The two bellhops, their bright blue uniforms already smudged from their efforts, took hold of the heavy trunk by the corners.

   —Amor Towles, *A Gentleman in Moscow*

   1. The little kids, their freshly laundered clothing nearly filthy from their playing, sat down on the muddy bank by the river.

   2. Its rays shining over the ocean, the sunset was enjoyed most nights by the people sitting or strolling on the Florida beach.

   3. A colorful bird, its startlingly red feathers very dazzling in their brightness, took off from the thick bush outside our window.

In the sentence-composing toolbox of good writers are three positions to add tools: *openers, splits, closers*. A sentence might also include a mix of these tools. The positions provide places to build better sentences like those of good writers, including famous authors.

The first version of the following paired sentences does not include tools. The second version does. As you read the paired sentences, notice how much more informative and powerful the second version is because of its use of tools.

OPENERS give your readers important information at the beginning of a sentence.

1a. Sloan seemed to care for only his daughter.

1b. A widower, Sloan seemed to care for only his daughter.

> —Langston Hughes, *The Big Sea*

2a. She plunged over the side of the boat.

2b. Kicking off her buckled shoes and dropping the woolen cloak, she plunged over the side of the boat.

> —Elizabeth George Speare, *The Witch of Blackbird Pond*

3a. All my dishes came crashing down.

3b. As my small back gave in to the mountainous weight, all my dishes came crashing down.

> —Kelly Yang, *Front Desk*

4a. I packed my suitcase and told my mother I was going to run away from home.

4b. **When I was in elementary school,** I packed my suitcase and told my mother I was going to run away from home.

>   —Jean Craighead George, *My Side of the Mountain*

SPLITS give your readers important details after the beginning of the sentence but before the end of the sentence. They split the subject from the predicate.

5a. The other pill came up again promptly along with the bowl of soup she'd forced down earlier.

5b. The other pill, **an aspirin she got down the boy's throat with great difficulty,** came up again promptly along with the bowl of soup she'd forced down earlier.

>   —Katherine Paterson, *The Great Gilly Hopkins*

6a. The hangman was waiting beside the gallows.

6b. The hangman, **a grey-haired convict in the white uniform of the prison,** was waiting beside the gallows.

>   —George Orwell, "A Hanging" (adapted)

7a. The creatures were all watching him intently.

7b. The creatures, **some sitting on chairs and others reclining on a sofa,** were all watching him intently.

>   —Roald Dahl, *James and the Giant Peach*

8a. Henry rushed out of his cabin.

8b. Henry, **when his shaking had stopped a little,** rushed out of his cabin.

>   —John Steinbeck, *Cannery Row*

CLOSERS give your readers important details at the closing of the sentence.

9a. The dictionary had a picture of an aardvark.

9b. The dictionary had a picture of an aardvark, **a long-tailed, long-eared, burrowing African mammal living off termites caught by sticking out its tongue as an anteater does for ants.**

> —Malcolm X and Alex Haley, *The Autobiography of Malcolm X*

10a. She trailed her fingers through the flour.

10b. She trailed her fingers through the flour, **parting and separating small hills and ridges of it to look for mites.**

> —Toni Morrison, *Beloved* (adapted)

11a. The dragon snarled his fearsome snarl.

11b. The dragon snarled his fearsome snarl, **his forked tongue hanging between teeth almost as long as fence pickets.**

> —Stephen King, *The Eyes of the Dragon*

12a. All the trouble began.

12b. All the trouble began **when my grandfather died and my grandmother came to live with us.**

> —Frank O'Connor, "First Confession"

MIXES give your readers important details in more than one place within a sentence.

13a. She sat in a rocking chair.

13b. A beautiful college student, she sat in a rocking chair, **looking very calm and composed**. (*Contains an opener and a closer.*)

—Michael Crichton, Travels (adapted)

14a. Alfy Simkins came home from football practice every evening bruised and aching.

14b. Alfy Simkins, **a roommate of yours,** came home from football practice every evening bruised and aching, **his hand scarcely able to shovel the mashed potatoes into his mouth**. (*Contains a split and a closer.*)

—Paul Roberts, "How to Say Nothing in Five Hundred Words" (adapted)

15a. Everybody for a hundred yards stared.

15b. When the snake wrangler pulled out the plywood boxes with snakes out of the station wagon, everybody for a hundred yards stared, **snapping their heads around at the sound**. (*Contains an opener and a closer.*)

—Michael Crichton, Travels (adapted)

Coming up are the most important activities in this worktext because they will help you learn, practice, imitate, and compose strong sentences built with openers, splits, closers, and mixes. After carefully doing those activities, you can build your sentences like the sentences of authors.

You'll never get anywhere with all
those little short sentences.

—Gregory Clark, *A Social Perspective on the Function of Writing*

OPENERS: GOOD BEGINNINGS

To give your readers important information at the beginning of a sentence, use openers. Here are pairs of sentences without openers and then with openers.

Directions: Tell how the added information in the opener improves the sentence.

1a. He went home and stood in front of the painting of his father.

1b. When Manolo heard them say how very much he looked like his father, he went home and stood in front of the painting of his father.

> —Maia Wojciechowska, *Shadow of a Bull* (adapted)

2a. She was even more **exquisite** [*beautiful*] than the doll he'd made for the infant Empress.

2b. The size of a five-year-old girl, she was even more exquisite than the doll he'd made for the infant Empress.

> —Kirby Larson, *The Friendship Doll*

3a. He considered running after her to explain himself.

3b. Wringing out the cold coffee from his shirt, he considered running after her to explain himself.

> —Sandhya Menon, *When Dimple Met Rishi* (adapted)

4a. I was standing alone in a cold and rainy night.

4b. The heavy door sliding shut, my fingernails moving along the splintery wood in a desperate effort to stop it, I was standing alone in a cold and rainy night.

> —Jack Finney, "Of Missing Persons"

ACTIVITY 1: MATCHING

Directions: At the caret (^), add the opener to the sentence it belongs to. Copy and punctuate the sentence.

Sentence	Opener
1. ^ , the teacher gave the class an assignment. —Lorenz Graham, "South Town"	**a.** The biggest reader of the three children
2. ^ , I thought it would be funny to jump into her shot. —Kelly Yang, *Front Desk*	**b.** When it was my mom's turn to take her photo
3. ^ , Tom Black has ridden nine horses to death in the rodeo arena. —Hal Borland, *When the Legends Die*	**c.** Twisting and punching and kicking
4. ^ , Klaus was the most likely to know vocabulary words and foreign phrases. —Lemony Snicket, *The Bad Beginning*	**d.** His hands raw
5. ^ , the two boys rolled across the floor. —Lois Duncan, *A Gift of Magic*	**e.** Cupping his hands tightly around his lips
6. ^ , he pitched the call high enough to make it sound like a young turkey gobbling. —Virginia Hamilton, *M. C. Higgins, the Great*	**f.** Her heart hammering in her chest
7. ^ , she ducked behind the nearest concrete pillar and peered around it. —Cassandra Clare, *City of Bones*	**g.** Before the bell rang
8. ^ , he finally reached a flat place at the top. —Richard Connell, "The Most Dangerous Game"	**h.** A veteran **bronco** [*wild horse*] rider

ACTIVITY 2: IDENTIFYING OPENERS

Directions: Openers are sentence parts, not complete sentences. In each of the following groups, find the only one that could not be an opener because it is a complete sentence, not a sentence part.

EXAMPLE

Sentence: ^ , king cobras rear and produce a hood around their heads.

1. **When they are threatened or disturbed**, king cobras rear and produce a hood around their heads.

2. **The world's largest poisonous snakes**, king cobras rear and produce a hood around their heads.

3. **These snakes are found in rain forests in India, southern China, and southeast Asia**, king cobras rear and produce a hood around their heads.

4. **Injecting often deadly poison into their prey**, king cobras rear and produce a hood around their heads.

5. **Their length reaching between thirteen and eighteen feet**, king cobras rear and produce a hood around their heads.

ANSWER: Number 3 is a sentence, not a sentence part. The rest are sentence parts.

----

1. *Sentence:* ^ , a horseshoe crab lives in the shallow waters of beaches.
   a. After it digs a hole where it will lay its eggs

   b. A prehistoric animal shaped like its name

   c. Coming ashore to lay its eggs

   d. The number of eggs is between 60,000 and 120,00

   e. Their eggs eaten by shore birds before the eggs hatch

2. *Sentence:* ^ , the Statue of Liberty now stands on Ellis Island in New York City's harbor.

   a. After it had been built in France and shipped to the United States

   b. A symbol of the United States of America

   c. Welcoming generations of immigrants

   d. The statue was built in France

   e. Her right hand holding a torch above her head

3. *Sentence:* ^ , Halloween is a holiday mostly for children.

   a. Children ring doorbells to ask for treats

   b. Although some adults also dress up in costumes

   c. A day when children dress up in costumes

   d. Coming each year on October 31

   e. Their costumes often based upon famous characters

4. *Sentence:* ^ , New York City attracts people from around the world.

   a. Although some Americans have never been there

   b. A famous city for American entertainment and culture

   c. One of its many attractions is the World Trade Center

   d. Boasting Times Square's bright neon and Broadway plays

   e. Its neighborhoods reflecting diverse cultures

5. *Sentence:* ^ , Alexander Hamilton rose from poverty to power.

   a. Although he had many hardships to overcome

   b. The subject of a popular musical

   c. He was shot and killed by Aaron Burr in a duel

   d. Growing up an orphan in the West Indies

   e. His reputation based on his intelligence and hard work

ACTIVITY 3: CHOOSING OPENERS

Directions: Following are sentences with the opener removed. Underneath are four openers (sentence parts) that could begin the sentence. Choose two you like. In two separate sentences, write out your two choices.

On the Mark: Put a comma after the opener.

EXAMPLE

Sentence: ^, she slammed her book down so hard the cat leaped off the table.

Openers:

    a. After her brother snuck up behind her and then screamed to scare her

    b. A hothead whose temper often got her into trouble

    c. Jumping up in a rage

    d. Her temper reaching the boiling point from the insult

Author's Sentence: When I told her what Grandpa said, she slammed her book down so hard the cat leaped off the table.

    —Olive Ann Burns, *Cold Sassy Tree*

---

1. ^ , he saw a movement on the ground, heard a scraping sound, and saw a rat take its head out of a paper bag and look at him.
    —John Cheever, "The Five-Forty-Eight"

    a. A wandering child hoping to see the rodent again

    b. Looking ahead and behind and left and right

    c. His mind on what had happened the hour before

    d. As he looked down

2. ^ , I was put in a special seat in the first row by the window, apart from the other children so that the teacher could tutor me without disturbing them.

—Julia Alvarez, "Snow"

    a. A new student in the class

    b. Looking around me at the other students

    c. My chin tucked down so that my face didn't show

    d. Because I was new to this school

3. ^ , I made it to the hotel desk.

—Wallace Stegner, *Crossing to Safety*

    a. An exhausted tourist who had gotten lost in the city

    b. Hoping to find a safe and comfortable place

    c. My nerves in terrible shape from the crowd outside

    d. Although I was more tired than I realized

4. ^ , I fought tears in my eyes.

—Kelly Yang, *Front Desk*

    a. Perhaps an overly sensitive person

    b. Trying unsuccessfully to feel okay

    c. My feelings hurt by what they had said

    d. After I thought about what had happened

ACTIVITY 4: EXCHANGING OPENERS

Directions: Replace the opener with one of your own about the same length as the original opener. Begin yours with the same word as the original opener.

EXAMPLE

Original Opener:

His hand trembling, Billy laid the peanut-butter-and-fried-worm sandwich down on the table.

—Thomas Rockwell, *How to Eat Fried Worms*

Possible Opener:

His stomach upset, Billy laid the peanut-butter-and-fried-worm sandwich down on the table. (*Many other openers are possible.*)

1. **When we got to the photo booth**, my mother's face lit up. (*In your opener, tell another time the mother's face lit up. Begin with* When.)

   —Kelly Yang, *Front Desk*

2. **A short, round boy of seven**, he took little interest in troublesome things, preferring to remain on good terms with everyone. (*In your opener, identify the boy in a new way. Begin with* A.)

   —Mildred D. Taylor, *Roll of Thunder, Hear My Cry*

3. **Carrying a bottle of milk**, Fern sat down under the apple tree inside the yard. (*In your opener, tell what else Fern might have carried. Begin with* Carrying.)

   —E. B. White, *Charlotte's Web*

4. **Her feet touching the side of the stone tower,** Violet closed her eyes and began to climb. (*In your opener, tell what else Violet might have been doing while climbing. Begin with* Her.)

—Lemony Snickett, The Bad Beginning (adapted)

ACTIVITY 5: ADDING AN OPENER

Directions: Following are sentences with the opener removed. Using any kind of opener, add your own.

EXAMPLE

Sentence: ^ , the creature screamed a loud and piteous whining and beat the ground with his palms.

—Lloyd Alexander, The Book of Three

Samples:

    a. Before the warrior had time to fire a second arrow, . . .

    b. A monster with five eyes struck in one of them by the arrow, . . .

    c. Leaping through the air to attack the huntsman, . . .

    d. Its five arms waving in agonizing pain, . . .

Original sentence: Rolling his eyes in confusion and shock, the creature screamed a loud and piteous whining and beat the ground with his palms.

1. ^ , the Laughing Man was kidnapped in infancy by bandits.

—J. D. Salinger, "The Laughing Man"

2. ^ , Taran leaped to his feet and plunged into the jungle.

—Lloyd Alexander, The Book of Three

3. ^ , they stood in a half circle around a hole in the ground, silent as stones.

> —Keith Donohue, *The Stolen Child*

4. ^ , the dragon released huge clouds of hissing steam through its nostrils.

> —Heywood Broun, "The Fifty-First Dragon"

ACTIVITY 6: UNSCRAMBLING TO IMITATE

Directions: Unscramble the sentence parts to imitate the model sentence. Start with the first sentence part listed. Write out the imitation sentence and <u>underline</u> the opener.

On the Mark: Put commas where they appear in the model.

EXAMPLE

Model Sentence: A small man, he wore a cotton shirt and a long, bloodstained smock.

> —Christopher Paolini, *Eragon*

SENTENCE PARTS TO UNSCRAMBLE TO IMITATE THE MODEL SENTENCE:

a. (*Start here.*) The fastest hunters

b. and four hard, rubbery feet

c. cheetahs

d. have a flexible spine

Imitation Sentence: <u>The fastest hunters</u>, cheetahs have a flexible spine and four hard, rubbery feet.

----

1. *Model Sentence:* As he looked through his porthole glass, he saw a wall of ice glide by.

   > —Walter Lord, *A Night to Remember*

   a. (*Start here.*) When Labelle searched in her crowded purse

   b. sink deeper

   c. she felt a bottle of perfume

2. *Model Sentence:* A real tear, it trickled down his shabby velvet nose and fell to the ground.

   > —Margery Williams, *The Velveteen Rabbit*

   a. (*Start here.*) A gentle smile

   b. across her freckled childlike face

   c. and lit up the room

   d. it spread

3. *Model Sentence:* Hobbling on one foot, Wanda opened the closet door and turned on the light.

   > —Betsy Byars, *The Summer of the Swans*

   a. (*Start here.*) Darting from its protective shelter

   b. reached the sky

   c. the bat

   d. and disappeared into the night

4. *Model Sentence:* Its head resting on one of the man's feet, on the floor was an old white English bull terrier.

   > —Sheila Burnford, *The Incredible Journey* (adapted)

a. (*Start here.*) Its shell steaming from the kettle of just boiled seafood

b. was

c. on the plate

d. a delicious Maryland blue crab

ACTIVITY 7: COMBINING TO IMITATE

Directions: Combine the **bold** parts into just one sentence that imitates the model. Copy the model sentence and the imitation sentence and <u>underline the opener in each</u>.

On the Mark: Put commas where they appear in the model.

EXAMPLE

Model Sentence: Holding a dozen tea glasses on a silver tray, she appeared at the entrance to the living room.

—Roya Hakakian, *Journey from the Land of No*

SENTENCES TO COMBINE TO IMITATE THE MODEL SENTENCE:

a. She was **carrying a brand-new tennis racquet in a leather case.**

b. She walked.

c. Her walk went **past the clubhouse.**

d. Her walk went **to the tennis court**.

Model Sentence: <u>Holding a dozen tea glasses on a silver tray</u>, she appeared at the entrance to the living room.

Imitation Sentence: <u>Carrying a brand-new tennis racquet in a leather case</u>, she walked past the clubhouse to the tennis court.

----

1. *Model Sentence:* As I think back on my life for the last thirty years, I admit I made some extremely poor decisions.
   —Ayn Rand, *Anthem*

   a. Something happens **when I look forward to my career**.

   b. The career is **after high school**.

   c. **I know I want** something.

   d. What I want is **a challenging steady occupation**.

2. *Model Sentence:* A weary old man, he stepped off the porch and with heavy footsteps and a heavier heart started the hike back to the car.
   —William P. Young, *The Shack*

   a. He was **a curious young scientist**.

   b. **He walked over the field.**

   c. **And with increasing speed and a determined mind** he walked.

   d. He **continued his study deep into the woods**.

3. *Model Sentence:* Jumping up, he pulled T. J. up, too, and he hit him **squarely** [*hard*] in the face.
   —Mildred D. Taylor, *Roll of Thunder, Hear My Cry*

   a. He was **climbing down**.

   b. While climbing down, **he helped Christina down, too**.

   c. **And he put her safely**.

   d. He put her **under the shelter**.

4. *Model Sentence:* His fingers **smarting** [*hurting*], the **shamefaced** [*embarrassed*] Taran hurried from the cottage and found Coll near the vegetable garden.
   —Lloyd Alexander, *The Book of Three*

a. This is what happened as **his legs** were **straining**.

b. What happened is that **the young athlete ran**.

c. He ran **around the track**.

d. And he **played music through his tiny earphones**.

ACTIVITY 8: IMITATING SENTENCES WITH OPENERS

Directions: Write an imitation sentence about something you saw on TV, on the Internet, or in a movie. Read the model sentence below, then its imitation, then your imitation. If all three are built pretty much alike, congratulations!

Tip: To help you, here is each sentence part of the model and its imitation part.

Model Sentence Parts	Imitation Sentence Parts
1. a. When I awoke,	**a.** As I drifted,
b. snowflakes	**b.** memories
c. were in my eyes. —Charles Portis, *True Grit*	**c.** danced in my mind.
2. a. A thoroughbred of the streets,	**a.** An expert in computer games,
b. Jemmy	**b.** Sheila
c. acted on instinct. —Sid Fleischman, *The Whipping Boy*	**c.** counted on experience.
3. a. Lying on the floor	**a.** Sitting in the chair
b. with the guns beside me,	**b.** with the rats around him,
c. I was wet, cold, and very hungry. —Ernest Hemingway, *A Farewell to Arms* (adapted)	**c.** he was shocked, disgusted, and totally terrified.

4. a. My eyes still shut,	**a.** His body fully ready,
b. I heard him bounce in through my bedroom door	**b.** we saw him turn around on the gym floor
c. and plop down on Jermaine's old bed. —David Barclay Moore, *The Stars Beneath Our Feet*	**c.** and jump up toward the basketball hoop.

QUIZ: OPENERS

Directions: Jot down whether the statement is true or false.

1. All of these but one could be an opener.

    • when the puppy appeared inside the gift box

    • a tiny puppy that could fit in your hand

    • the puppy curled up in her lap

    • licking the baby's outstretched hand

    • its fur soft as velvet

2. Openers are sentence parts, not complete sentences.

3. A comma is needed at the end of an opener.

4. This sentence has no opener:

    A single wrong note on the piano makes me want to hurl the score across the room.

    —Perri Knize, *Grand Obsession: A Piano Odyssey*

5. The opener is the longest part of this sentence:

    After the usual time of the exercise in meditation passed, Govinda rose.

    —Hermann Hesse, *Siddhartha*

PUTTING OPENERS TO WORK

Directions: Pair openers with sentences. Copy the paragraph about Cleopatra while inserting at the carets (^) the appropriate openers, listed out of order below.

CLEOPATRA

1. ^, Cleopatra ruled Egypt for twenty-two years. (2) ^, she lost a kingdom once, regained it, nearly lost it again, **amassed** [*built*] an empire, lost it all. (3) ^, she was an object of **speculation** [*guesswork*] and **veneration** [*respect*], gossip and legend, even in her own time. (4) ^, she controlled virtually the entire eastern Mediterranean coast, the last great kingdom of any Egyptian ruler.

   —Stacy Schiff, *Cleopatra: A Life* (adapted)

OPENERS:

a. Becoming a goddess as a child, a queen at eighteen, a celebrity soon after

b. Her rule a series of successes and failures

c. A contender for the most famous woman to have lived

d. When she was at the top of her power

QUESTION: What are three ways the paragraph with openers is better than the paragraph without openers?

SPLITS: GOOD ADDITIONS

To give your readers important information in the middle of a sentence, use splits. Here are pairs of sentences without splits and then with splits.

Directions: In the second sentence, tell how the added information in the split improves the sentence.

1a. The dog made a dash for the condemned prisoner and tried to lick his face.

1b. The dog, **before anyone could stop it**, made a dash for the condemned prisoner and tried to lick his face.

> —George Orwell, "A Hanging" (adapted)

2a. The fifth traveler napped upon his cane.

2b. The fifth traveler, **an old gentleman sitting next to the middle door across the aisle**, napped upon his cane.

> —Henry Sydnor Harrison, "Miss Hinch"

3a. The final exam would be given on Friday of the following week.

3b. The final exam, **covering a year's work in algebra**, would be given on Friday of the following week.

> —Jean Shepherd, *A Fistful of Fig Newtons*

4a. Tom looked out between the wheels.

4b. Tom, **his face already smudged with oil**, looked out between the wheels.

> —John Steinbeck, *The Grapes of Wrath*

ACTIVITY 1: MATCHING

Directions: At the caret (^), add the split to the sentence it belongs to. Copy and punctuate the sentence.

Sentence	Split
1. **Delicatessens** [*food stores*] on Sunday night, ^ , will overcharge you. —Saul Bellow, "A Father-to-Be"	**a.** as she stepped into the light
2. Her face, ^ , was round and thick with eyes like two **immense** [*huge*] eggs stuck into bread dough. —Ray Bradbury, *The Martian Chronicles* (adapted)	**b.** my new home
3. Anthocyanin, ^ , is produced by sugars that remain in the leaf after the supply of nutrients **dwindles** [*runs out*]. —Diane Ackerman, *A Natural History of the Senses*	**c.** swimming side by side
4. The living room of this house, ^ , is a sea of **beige** [*tan*] leather. —Ibi Zoboi, *American Street*	**d.** my nine-year-old brother
5. Four dolphins, ^ , were pushing the raft through the water. —Arthur C. Clarke, *Dolphin Island*	**e.** shouting and screaming
6. The children, ^ , came charging back into their homeroom. —Rosa Guy, *The Friends*	**f.** when all other stores are shut
7. Peter, ^ , is the only one of us happy with this turn of events. —Nicola Yoon, *The Sun Is Also a Star*	**g.** the pigment that gives apples their red and turns leaves red
8. A **seared** [*burned*] man, ^ , rose from the curb. —Fritz Leiber, "A Bad Day for Sales"	**h.** swimming side by side

ACTIVITY 2: IDENTIFYING SPLITS

Directions: Splits are sentence parts, not complete sentences. In each of the following groups, find the only one that could not be a split because it is a complete sentence, not a sentence part.

EXAMPLE

Sentence: Antarctica, ^ , is mostly uninhabited.

1. Antarctica, **because it is the coldest and windiest continent**, is mostly uninhabited.

2. Antarctica, **the fifth largest continent**, is mostly uninhabited.

3. Antarctica, **consisting of a covering of ice**, is mostly uninhabited.

4. Antarctica, **its environment too cold for most settlements to survive**, is mostly uninhabited.

5. Antarctica, **it is double the size of Australia**, is mostly uninhabited.

ANSWER: Number 5 is a sentence, not a sentence part. The rest are sentence parts.

----

1. *Sentence:* George Washington, ^ , is known as the father of the country.

   a. because he was its first president

   b. the commander of the Continental Army during the American Revolution

   c. living and dying at his home in Mount Vernon, Virginia

   d. his false teeth made of wood

   e. George was married to a woman named Martha

2. *Sentence:* Tarantulas, ^ , can appear outside North America as cobalt blue, or black with white stripes or yellow legs.

a. although most species in North America are brown

b. a form of hairy spider that some people make pets

c. the largest tarantulas have a leg span of almost twelve inches

d. varying in size from fingernail length to dinner plate size

e. their legs imprisoning their prey

3. *Sentence:* Many boats, ^ , were called into service for the evacuation of British soldiers from the French beach at Dunkirk.

   a. when the crisis of trapped soldiers on the beach became known

   b. a quickly assembled fleet of over 800 British ships

   c. rescuing 338,226 soldiers over an eight-day period

   d. their goal to rescue trapped British soldiers

   e. they were of all sizes and shapes

4. *Sentence:* The story of Dracula, ^ , has remained popular in novels and movies.

   a. because the original 1897 novel told a horrifying story that terrified but entertained readers

   b. many movies about Dracula don't follow the original 1897 story in the novel by Bram Stoker

   c. having been portrayed in over 250 films made in America and elsewhere

   d. his fang-like teeth enabling him to bite into the necks of victims and suck their blood

   e. the vampire villain portrayed in films by actor Bela Lugosi and others

5. *Sentence:* Walt Disney, ^, is the most famous entertainer in history.

   a. because he created an empire of highly successful movies and resorts

b. resorts with Disney character themes are found throughout the world

c. the recipient of a record 22 Academy Awards for his motion pictures

d. developing an interest in drawing at a young age

e. his creation of the character of Mickey Mouse in 1928 the beginning of many successful animated movies

ACTIVITY 3: CHOOSING SPLITS

Directions: Following are sentences with the split removed. Underneath are four splits (sentence parts) that could split the sentence. Choose two you like. In two separate sentences, write out your two choices.

On the Mark: Put a comma before and after the split.

EXAMPLE

Sentence: Manuel, ^ , was operated on.

Splits:

a. after he broke his neck during a fall in the mountains

b. a clumsy child having all kinds of accidents

c. having been attacked by a bear

d. his high temperature a serious problem

Author's Sentence: Manuel, the herder who shot himself in the foot, was operated on.

—Hal Borland, *When the Legends Die*

1. The first floor, ^, was where the rats lived.
> —Walter Dean Myers, *Motown and Didi*

a. after the rest of the house had been torn down

b. a sad reminder of what was once a beautiful house

c. sagging over the concrete foundation

d. its floorboards rotten and dangerous

2. Mrs. Klenk, ^ , lived in the basement five floors down.
> —Paula Fox, "Maurice's Room"

a. because she was the only disabled member of the apartment building

b. the mother of the twins who played with the other children

c. warning children to be especially careful on the cracked sidewalk

d. her voice irritating because of its loudness

3. His father, ^, started to cry.
> —Kate DiCamillo, *The Tiger Rising*

a. when he heard of the dog's death

b. the most upset member of the family

c. turning his face away from his children

d. his hands covering his eyes

4. An old barn, ^ , now was used as a garage.
> —Keith Donohue, *The Stolen Child*

a. when the farm had been sold to new owners

b. the children's favorite place to play

c. appearing much different because of the renovation

d. its stalls replaced by spaces for two cars

ACTIVITY 4: EXCHANGING SPLITS

Directions: Replace the split with one of your own about the same length as the author's original split. Begin yours with the same word as the original split.

EXAMPLE

Original Split:

I saw the big gray dog, **the leader of the wild pack**, in the brush above me.

Scott O'Dell, *Island of the Blue Dolphins*

Possible Split:

I saw the big gray dog, **the one that growled the loudest**, in the brush above me.

(Many other splits are possible.)

----

1. The poor fellow, **who looked thin and starved**, was sitting there trying to eat a bowl full of mashed-up green caterpillars without being sick. (*In your split, describe the fellow more. Begin with* who.)
   —Roald Dahl, *Charlie and the Chocolate Factory*

2. The face of Liliana Methol, **the fifth woman in the plane**, was badly bruised and covered with blood. (*In your split, identify her in a new way. Begin with* the.)

   —Piers Paul Read, *Alive*

3. Jody, **remembering how he had thrown the clod at the dog**, put his arm about the dog's neck and kissed him on his wide black nose. (*In your split, describe something else Jody could have remembered. Begin with* remembering.)

—John Steinbeck, The Red Pony

4. A large car, **its horn honking loudly**, sped through the intersection against the red light and roared directly toward the Hardys and Chet. (*In your split, tell what else the car might have been doing while speeding. Begin with* its.)

—Franklin W. Dixon, The Secret of the Old Mill

ACTIVITY 5: ADDING A SPLIT

Directions: Following are sentences with the split removed. Using any kind of split, add your own.

EXAMPLE

Sentence: The guitarist on the stage, ^ , let pure drops of sound fall into the noisy room.

—Lynne Rae Perkins, Criss Cross

Samples:

a. when he thought the time was right

b. a young muscular blonde

c. playing the notes sweetly

d. his thoughts on the upcoming chords

Original Sentence: The guitarist on the stage, tuning his guitar, let pure drops of sound fall into the noisy room.

1. The first thing she saw, ^, was a **hearse** [*vehicle carrying a coffin*].
   —Gaston Leroux, *The Phantom of the Opera*

2. One of their dogs, ^ , disappeared.
   —Fred Gipson, *Old Yeller*

3. A big kitchen table, ^ , was neatly set as if for a big party.
   —Robert Cormier, *Take Me Where the Good Times Are*

4. The small dragon, ^, wrapped its tail around the bedpost contentedly.
   —Christoper Paolini, *Eragon*

ACTIVITY 6: UNSCRAMBLING TO IMITATE

Directions: Unscramble the sentence parts to imitate the model sentence. Start with the first sentence part listed. Write out the imitation sentence and underline the split.

On the Mark: Put commas where they appear in the model.

EXAMPLE

Model Sentence: Marguerite Frolicher, a young Swiss girl accompanying her father on a business trip, woke up with a memory of her bad dream.

—Walter Lord, *A Night to Remember*

SENTENCE PARTS TO UNSCRAMBLE TO IMITATE THE MODEL SENTENCE:

a. (*Start here.*) Harry Houdini

b. became famous for an escape from an underwater box

c. entertaining his audiences with many amazing tricks

d. a famous Hungarian magician

Imitation Sentence: Harry Houdini, <u>a famous Hungarian</u> <u>magician entertaining his audiences with many amazing tricks,</u> became famous for an escape from an underwater box.

----

1. *Model Sentence:* Both Hardy boys, although they were uncomfortably wet, stayed to see what they could find out.

   —Franklin W. Dixon, *The Secret of the Old Mill*

   a. (*Start here*) Swarming monarch butterflies

   b. places they can be warm

   c. when they are migrating south

   d. travel to find

2. *Model Sentence:* Dr. John Lilly, the first scientist to attempt communication with dolphins, suggested ways that **clarified** [*explained*] dolphin communication.

   —Arthur C. Clarke, *Dolphin Island* (adapted)

   a. (*Start here.*) Henry Ford

   b. that revolutionized most manufacturing

   c. started improvements

   d. the only manufacturer to use assembly lines for cars

3. *Model Sentence:* The boy, straining in darkness when the lantern was dimmed so as not to alert the wood's creatures, picked out a **blurred** [*unclear*] shape in the dark.

   —William H. Armstrong, *Sounder* (adapted)

a. (*Start here.*) The doctor

b. so as not to upset the little kid

c. handed out a colored lollipop to the toddler

d. watching with care when the child was examined

4. *Model Sentence:* A thick scarf, its ends tucked into his coat, was crossed over his chest.

> —Leslie Norris, "Three Shots for Charlie Beston"

a. (*Start here.*) A broken wing

b. across its body

c. its feathers damaged by a cat

d. was dangling

ACTIVITY 7: COMBINING TO IMITATE

Directions: Combine the **bold** parts into just one sentence that imitates the model. Copy the model sentence and the imitation sentence and underline the split in each.

On the Mark: Put commas where they appear in the model.

EXAMPLE

Model Sentence: Four dolphins, swimming side by side, were pushing the raft through the water.

> —Arthur C. Clarke, *Dolphin Island*

SENTENCES TO COMBINE TO IMITATE THE MODEL SENTENCE:

a. There were **several bats**.

b. They were **flying through the yard.**

c. The bats **were hunting the insects**.

d. The insects were **over the lawn**.

Model Sentence: Four dolphins, <u>swimming side by side</u>, were pushing the raft through the water.

Imitation Sentence: Several bats, <u>flying through the yard</u>, were hunting the insects over the lawn.

---

1. *Model Sentence:* Lesley, when she felt the lawn mower bearing down on her, abandoned her half of the wide handle and leaped out of the way.

   —Lynne Reid Banks, *One More River*

   a. Houdini did something.

   b. He did it **because he experienced the water pressure holding tight on him**.

   c. He **signaled his trainer near the glass cage**.

   d. And he **pounded hard on the glass**.

2. *Model Sentence:* The night of my engagement, the night Peeta fell to his knees and spoke his everlasting love for me, was the night the rebellion began.

   —Suzanne Collins, *Catching Fire* (adapted)

   a. It was **the day of the bombing**.

   b. It was **the day Japan flew over Pearl Harbor**.

   c. And the day Japan **bombed the unsuspecting boats in harbors**.

   d. That **was the day the war began**.

3. *Model Sentence:* Arthur Peuchen, starting to undress for the night, thought the sound of the *Titanic* hitting the iceberg was like a train crash.

> —Walter Lord, *A Night to Remember*

   a. This is about **Ricky Martinez**.

   b. He was **trying to sleep during the night**.

   c. He **thought the whoosh of the wind rattling the shutters was like** something.

   d. It was like **a scary movie**.

4. *Model Sentence:* The small dragon, its eyes closed, wrapped its tail around the bedpost contentedly.

> —Christopher Paolini, *Eragon*

   a. **The prehistoric animal** did something.

   b. **Its skin** was **scaled**.

   c. It **darted its tongue**.

   d. It darted it **toward the dinosaur menacingly**.

ACTIVITY 8: IMITATING SENTENCES WITH SPLITS

Directions: Write an imitation sentence about something you saw on TV, on the Internet, or in a movie. Read the model sentence in the following chart, then its imitation, then your imitation. If all three are built pretty much alike, congratulations!

> **Tip:** To help you, here is each sentence part of the model and its imitation.

Model Sentence Parts	Imitation Sentence Parts
1. a. The truck drivers,	**a.** The police officers,
b. when they heard that Maxie had been released,	**b.** when they saw that demonstrators had been cleared,
c. were furious. —Jean Merrill, *The Pushcart War*	**c.** were relieved.
2. a. Sarah,	**a.** Manuel,
b. a thin woman who wears denims and cowboy boots,	**b.** an athletic guy who plays basketball and football,
c. runs a falling-apart post office. —Truman Capote, *In Cold Blood* (adapted)	**c.** heads a super-popular sports club.
3. a. Sophie,	**a.** Rodrigo,
b. sitting on the Big Friendly Giant's hand,	**b.** surfing the ocean's waves,
c. peeped out of the cave. —Roald Dahl, *The BFG*	**c.** rode on top of them.
4. a. A man in furs,	**a.** A snake in the meadow,
b. his face hidden in the deep hood of his **garment** [*clothes*],	**b.** its movements unseen in the tall grass of the field,
c. stood in the **foreground** [*front*]. —Philip Pullman, *The Golden Compass*	**c.** crawled near the cat.

QUIZ: SPLITS

Directions: Jot down whether the statement is true or false.

1. All of these but one could be a split.

   - when the runner rounded third base heading home

   - a pitcher famous for hurling the ball like lightning

   - tying the game in the bottom of the eighth inning

   - the crowd cheered the team

   - their coach after their win jumping up and down

2. Splits are sentences, not sentence parts.

3. Only one comma is needed for a split.

4. This sentence has no split.

   > *His target, a small doe with a pronounced limp in her left forefoot, was still with the herd.*

   > —Christopher Paolini, *Eragon*

5. The split is the shortest part of this sentence.

   > *The neighbor's dog weirdly named Rosie, a male boxer, lifted his leg on the dining-room table and sprayed the white tablecloth with urine.*

   > —Kate DiCamillo, *The Miraculous Journey of Edward Tulane*
   > (adapted)

PUTTING SPLITS TO WORK

Directions: Pair splits with sentences. Copy the paragraph about the drowning nightmare while inserting at the carets (^) the appropriate splits, listed out of order below:

DROWNING

(1) In my nightmare Chris and I, ^ , were out over our heads in water. (2) Suddenly Chris's head, ^ , went under. (3) Under the water two bloated corpses, ^ , were holding his ankles. (4) The lifeguard, ^, just went on smiling down at a girl in a red bathing suit. (5) Chris's scream, ^ , turned into a bubbling water-choked gurgle. (6) A soft, rotted hand, ^ , began to pull. (7) Suddenly the nightmare washed away. (8) My brother, ^ , had his hand on my leg.

—Stephen King, "The Body" (adapted)

SPLITS:

a. his tanned body posing attractively on his high seat

b. his mouth filling with water

c. swimming lazily along in a hot July sun

d. shaking me awake

e. as the corpses pulled him further under

f. their open eyes as white as the eyes of statues

g. wrapping itself around my leg

QUESTION: What are three ways the paragraph with splits is better than the paragraph without splits?

CLOSERS: GOOD ENDINGS

To give your readers important information at the end of a sentence, use closers. Here are pairs of sentences without closers and then with closers.

Directions: In the second sentence, tell how the added information in the closer improves the sentence.

1a. I was just fourteen years of age.

1b. I was just fourteen years of age, **when a coward named Tom Chaney shot my father.**

> —Charles Portis, *True Grit* (adapted)

2a. This was Albany.

2b. This was Albany, **the capital of the state of New York.**

> —E. L. Konigsburg, *The View from Saturday*

3a. The dog was making an awful noise.

3b. The dog was making an awful noise, **a half-strangled mixture of growl and bark.**

> —William H. Armstrong, *Sounder*

4a. Thankfully, Mamma returned then.

4b. Thankfully, Mamma returned then, **her arms trembling from holding a heavy silver tray laden with a teapot, teacups, and cookies and plates.**

> —Sandhya Menon, *When Dimple Met Rishi*

ACTIVITY 1: MATCHING

Directions: At the caret (^), add the closer to the sentence it belongs to. Copy and punctuate the sentence.

Sentence	Closer
1. Dr. Strauss might be called a genius, ^ . —Daniel Keyes, *Flowers for Algernon*	**a.** an old .44 Winchester and much too small to kill an elephant
2. He was running all-out now and **dodged** [*avoided*] tree trunks and low-hanging branches ^ . —Robert Ludlum, *The Moscow Vector*	**b.** his chest **punctured** [*wounded*]
3. The dictionary had a picture of an aardvark, ^ . —Malcolm X and Alex Haley, *The Autobiography of Malcolm X*	**c.** his little body **quivering** [*shaking*] with fear in the great open sun on the **blazing** [*hot*] concrete
4. I took my rifle, ^ . —George Orwell, "Shooting an Elephant" (adapted)	**d.** although I felt that his areas of knowledge were too limited
5. Children love to play in piles of leaves, ^ . —Diane Ackerman, *A Natural History of the Senses*	**e.** **hurling** [*throwing*] them into the air like confetti, leaping into soft mattresses of them
6. Almost everything I have now has already been thrown out at least once, ^ . —Lars Eighner, "On Dumpster Diving"	**f.** proving that what I own is **valueless** [*worthless*] to someone
7. I saw the mouse vanish in the general direction of my apartment house, ^ . —Loren Eiseley, "The Brown Wasps"	**g.** as they **loomed up** [*appeared*] suddenly in front of him

(*continues*)

(continued)

Sentence	Closer
8. The soldier **arched** [*fell*] backward, ^ . —Robert Ludlum, *The Prometheus Deception*	h. a long-tailed, long-eared, burrowing African mammal living off termites caught by sticking out its tongue as an anteater does for ants

ACTIVITY 2: IDENTIFYING CLOSERS

Directions: Closers are sentence parts, not complete sentences. In each of the following groups, find the only one that could not be a closer because it is a complete sentence, not a sentence part.

EXAMPLE

> *Sentence:* Nelson Mandela committed himself to ending apartheid, ^ .

1. Nelson Mandela committed himself to ending apartheid **when he was a young man.**

2. Nelson Mandela committed himself to ending apartheid, **a system of racial segregation that gave white people privileges in Africa.**

3. Nelson Mandela committed himself to ending apartheid, **becoming involved in anti-colonial politics.**

4. Nelson Mandela committed himself to ending apartheid, **he was the first president of South Africa.**

5. Nelson Mandela committed himself to ending apartheid, **his long imprisonment finally rewarded with the elimination of apartheid.**

ANSWER: Number 4 is a sentence, not a sentence part. The rest are sentence parts.

----

1. *Sentence:* Hyenas are frequently viewed as frightening and worthy of contempt, ^ .

   a. although they feature prominently in folklore and mythology

   b. their body parts used as medicine in Somalia

   c. hyenas were villains in Disney's movie *The Lion King*

   d. stealing and eating livestock and sometimes even children

   e. their ability to play dead effective in keeping enemy animals away

2. *Sentence:* The Bermuda Triangle has been a source of fascination, ^ .

   a. because the mysteries that surround it have never been completely explained

   b. a location where planes and boats have mysteriously disappeared

   c. upsetting superstitious persons but attracting scientific investigators

   d. its waters the area of unexplained disappearances of planes and boats

   e. it is an area where some pilots refuse to fly

3. *Sentence:* President Kennedy was assassinated, ^.

   a. although he was a very popular leader

   b. a shocking event in twentieth-century American history

   c. leaving behind a wife and two small children

   d. his wife's bloody jacket becoming a horrible symbol of the event

   e. the vice president had to take over running the country

4. *Sentence:* The seahorse is a tropical fish, ^ .

   a. because it needs warm water to survive and multiply

    b. a small fish named for its appearance like a horse

    c. seahorses rely on camouflage with their surroundings to avoid detection

    d. reversing the usual pattern because the male carries the babies in a pouch

    e. its head the reason for its name

5. Sentence: The United Nations intends to maintain peace among global nations, ^ .

    a. because the organization was created after World War II in the hope of preventing another war

    b. a complicated but worthwhile international organization founded in 1945

    c. promoting human rights and fostering humanitarian goals

    d. its headquarters in New York City on eighteen acres along the East River

    e. its name was created by United States President Franklin D. Roosevelt

ACTIVITY 3: CHOOSING CLOSERS

Directions: Following are sentences with the closer removed. Underneath are four closers (sentence parts) that could end the sentence. Choose two you like. In two separate sentences, write out your two choices.

On the Mark: Put a comma before the closer.

EXAMPLE

Sentence: Inside the box was something her mother had always wanted for her, ^ .

Closers:

a. although she was not sure how she would respond

b. a pair of ballet slippers

c. shining from the bright, metallic wrapping paper

d. its wrapping paper completely hiding the contents of the package

Author's Sentence: Inside the box was something her mother had always wanted for her, a silk **kimono** [*robe*] with cherry blossoms on it.

—Eleanor Coerr, *Sadako and the Thousand Paper Cranes*

----

1. Halfway there he heard the sound he dreaded, ^ .

    —John Steinbeck, *The Red Pony*

    a. since that sound meant that the struggle was ending

    b. a series of long wheezing gasps for air

    c. filling his mind with the sound he hoped never to hear

    d. the high-pitched scream of a woman who has just discovered a corpse

2. Higher and higher the wave rose, ^ .

    —Armstrong Sperry, *Call It Courage*

    a. as the hurricane gained speed and power

    b. a wall of water that could not be escaped

    c. threatening to hit all the boats in the harbor

    d. its size and volume terrifying

3. Across his face there swept rigid surprise and then bursting agony, and then his scream rang out, ^ .

    —Bill and Vera Cleaver, *Where the Lilies Bloom*

a. as the ax fell

b. a force that threw the others backwards in shock

c. echoing repeatedly in the minds of witnesses

d. his accident too painful for the witnesses to continue watching

4. The huge head of the tyrannosaur raised back up, ^ .
   —Michael Crichton, *Jurassic Park*

a. as it peered into the window of our Jeep

b. an angry beast ready to attack

c. stopping near the place where the kids were hiding

d. its jaws open and roaring

ACTIVITY 4: EXCHANGING CLOSERS

Directions: Replace the closer with one of your own about the same length as the original closer. Begin yours with the same word as the original closer.

EXAMPLE

Original closer: Suddenly, Gollum sat down and began to weep, a whistling and gurgling sound horrible to listen to.

—J. R. R. Tolkien, *The Hobbit*

Possible Closer:

Suddenly, Gollum sat down and began to weep, a sad moan about the death of his pet goldfish.

(*Many other closers are possible.*)

1. His voice seemed sad, **although he was trying to be cheerful**. (*In your closer, tell what he did not to seem sad. Begin with* although.)

    —Theodore Taylor, *The Cay*

2. Sara watched him as he walked, **a small figure for his ten years with faded blue jeans and a striped knit shirt stretched out of shape.** (*In your closer, identify him in a new way. Begin with* a.)

    —Betsy Byars, *The Summer of the Swans*

3. He moved around to the rear of the car and was **rummaging** [*searching*] in the back of the station wagon, **looking at what looked like a bunch of junk to me.** (*In your closer, describe something else he could have been seeing. Begin with* looking.)

    —Gary Paulsen, *The Monument*

4. The dinosaur stood near the front of our car, **its chest moving as it breathed.** (*In your closer, tell what else the dinosaur might have been doing while standing near the car. Begin with* its.)

    —Michael Crichton, *Jurassic Park*

ACTIVITY 5: ADDING A CLOSER

Directions: Following are sentences with the closer removed. Using any kind of closer, add your own.

EXAMPLE

Sentence: The guitarist on the stage let pure drops of sound fall into the noisy room, ^ .

—Lynne Rae Perkins, *Criss Cross* (adapted)

SAMPLES:

    a. when he thought the time was right

    b. a hugely popular rock venue

    c. playing the notes sweetly

    d. his thoughts on the upcoming chords

    Original Sentence: The guitarist on the stage, tuning his guitar, let pure drops of sound fall into the noisy room.

---

1. A break in the clouds in a gray day threw a shaft of sunlight upon her coffin, ^ .

    —William Allen White, "Mary White"

2. After a few weeks Mother managed to buy me a new wheelchair, ^ .

    —Christy Brown, *My Left Foot*

3. Down a long road through the woods, a little boy **trudged** [*walked slowly*] to school, ^ .

    —Laura Ingalls Wilder, *Farmer Boy*

    —Christoper Paolini, *Eragon*

4. His mother sat sideways by the center fire, ^ .

ACTIVITY 6: UNSCRAMBLING TO IMITATE

Directions: Unscramble the sentence parts to imitate the model sentence. Start with the first sentence part listed. Write out the imitation sentence and underline the closer.

On the Mark: Put commas where they appear in the model.

EXAMPLE

Model Sentence: They walked through the thin snow to the row of heavy wooden rabbit **hutches** [*cages*], leaving dark footmarks on the hard frozen ground.

—Susan Cooper, *The Dark Is Rising*

SENTENCE PARTS TO UNSCRAMBLE TO IMITATE THE MODEL SENTENCE:

a. (*Start here.*) We

b. investigating any clues for the mysterious missing persons

c. to the area of lost American explorers

d. traveled though the Amazon forest

Imitation Sentence: We traveled though the Amazon forest to the area of lost American explorers, <u>investigating any clues for the mysterious missing persons</u>.

---

1. *Model Sentence:* She **festooned** [*decorated*] our living room in green and yellow streamers, the colors of my new school.

    —John Green, *Looking for Alaska*

    a. (*Start here.*) Children

    b. the sparks of every child's imagination

    c. with stars and lightning bugs

    d. watched the summer sky

2. *Model Sentence:* I unwrapped the present slowly, folding the paper carefully while slipping it off.

    —Sarah Dessen, *Dreamland*

    a. (*Start here.*) She

    b. while pulling it out

    c. digging the wound slowly

    d. withdrew the splinter carefully

3. *Model Sentence:* Kit could see the little wooden doll bobbing helplessly in the water, its arms sticking stiffly into the air.
    —Elizabeth George Speare, *The Witch of Blackbird Pond* (adapted)

    a. (*Start here.*) Rachel

    b. its legs pedaling hopefully under the water

    c. could see the little drowning chipmunk

    d. gasping frantically in the stream

4. *Model Sentence:* I was getting closer to nineteen every stinking day, while Edward stayed frozen in all his seventeen-year-old perfection as he had for over ninety years.
    —Stephenie Meyer, *Breaking Dawn*

    a. (*Start here*) The T. rex

    b. as they had for nearly several generations

    c. while others evolved slowly in all their less complicated forms

    d. was moving nearer to extinction every passing era

ACTIVITY 7: COMBINING TO IMITATE

Directions: Combine the **bold** parts into just one sentence that imitates the model. Copy the model sentence and the imitation sentence and underline the closer in each.

On the Mark: Put commas where they appear in the model.

EXAMPLE

Model Sentence: With a quick, guilty hand she covered the tear, her shoulders bunching to hide her face.

—Zenna Henderson, "The Believing Child"

SENTENCES TO COMBINE TO IMITATE THE MODEL SENTENCE:

a. **With a silent, sideways glance Jackson** did something.

b. He **signaled his partner**.

c. **His signal** was **aiming** to do something.

d. It was trying **to prevent the attack**.

Model Sentence: With a quick, guilty hand she covered the tear, her shoulders bunching to hide her face.

Imitation Sentence: With a silent, sideways glance Jackson signaled his partner, his signal aiming to prevent the attack.

---

1. *Model Sentence:* Walking was difficult, because both his knees were badly bruised and one ankle hurt with every step.
   —Alexander Key, *The Forgotten Door* (adapted)

   a. **Talking was impossible**

   b. It was impossible **because both his lips were completely swollen**.

   c. It was for that reason **and his jaw throbbed**.

   d. It throbbed **with every attempt**.

2. *Model Sentence:* Paddy became friendly with a cow from a nearby field, a big, fat, brown animal with sleepy eyes and an enormous tail that coiled about its hind legs like a rope.

—Christy Brown, *My Left Foot*

a. Suzie looked lovely **in her dress**.

b. The dress was **from the children's department**.

c. It was **a soft, lavender silk dress with white flowers and a large bow**.

d. It was a bow **that tied around her waist like a present**.

3. *Model Sentence:* She went back to the car, startling a flock of gulls that found a beached fish and were fighting over it.

—Katherine Paterson, *Park's Quest* (adapted)

a. Here is what **Santiago** did.

b. He **looked up at the mountains**.

c. He was **watching a cloud of ash**.

d. It was a cloud of ash **that threatened the hiker's trail and was spreading across it**.

4. *Model Sentence:* Big, rough teen-agers **jostled** [*pushed*] through the crowd, their sleeves rolled high to show off blue and red tattoos.

—Robert Lipsyte, *The Contender*

a. **Small, timid fish floated**.

b. They floated **within the ocean**.

c. **Their protective covering** was **turned on**.

d. They turned it on **to ward off large and nearby enemies**.

ACTIVITY 8: IMITATING SENTENCES WITH CLOSERS

Directions: Write an imitation sentence about something you saw on TV, on the Internet, or in a movie. Read the model sentence in the chart below, then its imitation, then your imitation. If all three are built pretty much alike, congratulations!

Tip: To help you, here is each sentence part of the model and its imitation part.

Model Sentence Parts	Imitation Sentence Parts
1. a. Many still died **b.** from the disease, **c.** although the atom bomb hit Hiroshima nine years before. —Eleanor Coerr, *Sadako and the Thousand Paper Cranes*	**a.** Crowds soon gathered **b.** for the parade, **c.** although the marching bands assembled floats several blocks away.
2. a. The cloudless sky **b.** turned a deep purple, **c.** the color of an old bruise. —George R. R. Martin, *Game of Thrones* (adapted)	**a.** The calm lake **b.** resembled a large mirror, **c.** a reflection of the blue sky.
3. a. The diggers gathered **b.** about the rim of the pit, **c.** staring. —Edmund Ware, "An Underground Episode"	**a.** The climbers rose **b.** to the top of the mountain, **c.** celebrating.
4. a. He carried the book **b.** with him in one hand, **c.** his pistol ready in the other. —Ray Bradbury, *The Martian Chronicles*	**a.** Smith took the hammer **b.** with him in his belt, **c.** his nails handy in his pocket.

QUIZ: CLOSERS

Directions: Jot down whether the statement is true or false.

1. All of these but one could be a closer.

   - because the rain stopped the game
   - a rookie who hit a homerun
   - the fans got excited
   - stealing second base
   - his bat flying through the air

2. Closers are sentence parts, not sentences.

3. A comma is needed before a closer.

4. This sentence has no closer.

   Sometimes I feel about eight years old, my body squeezed up and everything else tall.

   —Ray Bradbury, *The Martian Chronicles*

5. The closer is the longest part of this sentence.

   The six swans seemed motionless on the water, their necks all arched at the same angle so that it seemed there was only one swan mirrored five times.

   —Betsy Byars, *The Summer of the Swans*

PUTTING CLOSERS TO WORK

Directions: Pair closers with sentences. Copy the paragraph about the junkyard while inserting at the carets (^) the correct closers, listed out of order below:

JUNKYARD DOG

(1) There were plenty of animals at the dump, ^ . (2) There were plump rats feeding on rotting hamburger and maggoty vegetables. (3) It was also the place for stray dogs, ^ , ^ . (4) These dogs, though, never attacked Milo Pressman the dump-keeper, ^ , ^. (5) Some said Pressman's dog Chopper was a Doberman, ^ . (6) Pressman trained Chopper to **sic** [*attack*] specific body parts. (7) An unfortunate kid who **scaled** [*climbed*] the dump fence might hear Pressman cry, "Chopper! Sic! Hand!" (8) Chopper would grab that hand and hold on, ^ , ^ .

—Stephen King, *"The Body"* (adapted)

CLOSERS:

a. because Milo was never without Chopper

b. an ugly-tempered **lot** [*group*]

c. although they weren't the kind you see in the Walt Disney nature films

d. its vocal cords removed so you couldn't hear him when he was on the attack

e. attacking each other over a piece of bologna or a pile of chicken guts

f. ripping skin and tendons, powdering bones between his jaws

g. the most feared, meanest, ugliest dog around

QUESTION: What are three ways the paragraph with closers is better than the paragraphs without openers?

REVIEW: THE SENTENCE-COMPOSING POSITIONS

Congratulations on learning, practicing, and using these powerful sentence-composing positions: *opener*, *split*, *closer*. Like all good writers, you'll want to take them out of your sentence-composing toolbox to build strong sentences for just about everything you write.

One popular author is J. K. Rowling, who wrote the Harry Potter series. The following review activities show how she uses those positions in those stories.

REVIEW 1: NAMING THE POSITIONS

Directions: Find the tool and name its position in the sentence—*opener*, *split*, *closer*.

SOURCES:

1–5, *Harry Potter and the Sorcerer's Stone*

6–10, *Harry Potter and the Chamber of Secrets*

11–15, *Harry Potter and the Prisoner of Azkaban*

1. Ron stared after her, his mouth open.

2. Hiding something behind his back, Hagrid shuffled into view.

3. Neville, his face tear-streaked and clutching his wrist, hobbled off with Madame Hooch.

4. They heard something that made their hearts stop, a high, petrified scream coming from the chamber they'd just chained up.

5. When everyone had eaten as much as they could, the remains of the food **faded** [*disappeared*] from the plate.

6. Several people in green robes were walking onto the field, their broomsticks in their hands.

7. Their little shoulders bent, the crowd of gnomes in the field started walking away in a staggering line.

8. One of the owls, the large snowy female, was Harry's own Hedwig.

9. As warm blood drenched Harry's arms, he felt a **searing** [*sharp*] pain just above the elbow.

10. A jet of green light shot out of the wrong end of Ron's wand, hitting him in the stomach to send him reeling backward onto the grass.

11. Ernie Prang, an elderly wizard wearing very thick glasses, nodded to Harry.

12. Red Caps were nasty little creatures that lurked in the dungeons of castles and the battlefields, waiting to **bludgeon** [*beat up*] those who had gotten lost.

13. They looked up to see the Hogwarts Express, puffing smoke over a platform packed with witches and wizards seeing their children onto the train.

14. Harry sat down between Dudley and Uncle Vernon, a large beefy man with very little neck and a lot of mustache.

15. An **unearthly** [*creepy*] sound filled the room, a long, wailing shriek that made the hair on Harry's head stand on end.

REVIEW 2: IMITATING HARRY POTTER SENTENCES

Directions: For each model sentence from *Goblet of Fire*, choose a corresponding imitation sentence from the list below and write its letter in the margin. Then write your own imitation of the same model. The positions are underlined and named.

MODEL SENTENCES

1. The spider stretched its legs, then did a back flip, <u>landing on the desk</u>. (*CLOSER*)

2. <u>His powers gone and his life almost **extinguished** [*ended*]</u>, Voldemort fled. (*OPENER*)

3. A large wooden trunk was open at the foot of his bed, <u>revealing a cauldron, broomstick, black robes, and assorted spellbooks</u>. (*CLOSER*)

4. <u>While his magical eye swiveled around</u>, Moody began to call out names of students. (*OPENER*)

5. Voldemort, <u>the most powerful dark wizard for a century</u>, arrived at Harry's house and killed Harry's father and mother. (*SPLIT*)

IMITATION SENTENCES

A. Incas, the most sophisticated culture-builders of their time, created a powerful civilization and shared their wealth and knowledge.

B. The sun colored its rays, then showed a crimson circle, appearing over the horizon.

C. While its sticky thread imprisoned the insects, the spider crawled to eat up glued flies.

D. Her throat closing and her lungs nearly empty, Tawanda fainted.

E. A hidden secret door was opening in the dark of the attic, admitting a troll, ghost, dark wizard, and evil witch.

REVIEW 3: PARTNERING WITH J. K. ROWLING

Directions: At each caret (^) in the following Harry Potter sentences, add a sentence-composing tool good enough to be in a Harry Potter story!

1. ^ , the whole group seemed to hold its breath.
   >—*Order of the Phoenix*

2. He was wiping the same glass with the same **filthy** [*dirty*] rag, ^ .
   >—*Order of the Phoenix*

3. Harry, ^, bent back over his cauldron.
   >—*Half-Blood Prince*

4. ^ , Harry hurried off toward the store to find what he needed.
   >—*Half-Blood Prince*

5. Another friend of the family was Bathilda Bagshot, ^ .
   >—*Deathly Hallows*

6. ^, Dumbledore left Hogwarts in a blaze of glory.
   >—*Deathly Hallows*

MIXES: GOOD VARIETY

Mash-up, medley, assortment, combination, array, mixture, miscellany, potpourri, smorgasbord—they all mean variety.

The saying "Variety is the spice of life" applies also to sentences. The spice aisle in a food store has hundreds of different flavors— salt, pepper, turmeric, and cardamom—because people like flavor in their food.

In their sentences, too, people like flavor. A powerful way to add spice and flavor to sentences is in the mix, which includes a variety of positions you already know—*the opener, the split, the closer*—within the same sentence.

Read the following sentence pairs. The first sentence has no mix. The second has a mix that has more information, spice, and variety.

1a. Nellie sang Edward a lullaby.

1b. Nellie, <u>before she put him to bed each night</u>, sang Edward a lullaby, <u>a song about a mockingbird that did not sing and a diamond ring that would not shine</u>. (*Mix contains a split and a closer.*)

—Kate DiCamillo, *The Miraculous Journey of Edward Tulane*

2a. The tyrannosaur stood near the front of the Land Cruiser.

2b. <u>Its chest moving as it breathed</u>, the tyrannosaur stood near the front of the Land Cruiser, <u>its arms making clawing movements in the air</u>. (*Mix contains an opener and a closer.*)

—Michael Crichton, *Jurassic Park* (adapted)

3a. Charles Wallace looked very small.

3b. <u>When he sat there alone in the big old-fashioned kitchen</u>, Charles Wallace looked very small, <u>a blond little boy in faded blue denims</u>, <u>his feet swinging a good six inches above the floor</u>. (*Mix contains an opener and two closers.*)

—Madeleine L'Engle, *A Wrinkle in Time*

ACTIVITY 1: IDENTIFYING MIXES

Directions: Each sentence has a mix of two different positions. Copy the sentence, and underline and name each position in the mix.

EXAMPLE

Her dust rag in hand, my mother wandered by and stood in the doorway, listening carefully.

—Keith Donohue, *The Stolen Child*

<u>Her dust rag in hand</u>, my mother wandered by and stood in the doorway, <u>listening carefully</u>. (*OPENER, CLOSER*)

1. The only other person in the room, a husky young man with a broken nose, came over to Jelly, his hand outstretched.
   —Robert Lipsyte, *The Contender*

2. His book in his hand, Patrick was at another shelf, looking at soldiers of differing periods.
   —Lynne Reid Banks, *The Return of the Indian*

3. The scrub, a big wild stretch of dry and sandy land, was an unexplored wilderness, beckoning the children.
   —Lois Lenski, *Strawberry Girl*

4. Paintings of Alek's ancestors, the family who ruled Austria for six hundred years, lined the hallway, their faces staring down.
   —Scott Westerfeld, *Leviathan* (adapted)

5. As Count Olaf continued to brag, the youngest child peered into the jar, wondering how to make something interesting out of white beans and nothing else.
   —Lemony Snicket, *The End*

ACTIVITY 2: INSERTING MIXES

Directions: The mix has been removed from each sentence. A list of two sentence parts is underneath each sentence. Copy the sentence while adding the two sentence parts into two *different* positions. Underline and name the positions.

On the Mark: The sentence parts need commas to separate them from the rest of the sentence.

EXAMPLE

Shortened Sentence: The sled turned over.

> *Sentence Parts to Add:*
> - as they swung on the turn
> - spilling half its load

Sample Arrangement: (Others are possible.)

> <u>As they swung on the turn</u>, the sled, <u>spilling half its load</u>, turned over. (*OPENER, SPLIT*)

ORIGINAL SENTENCE:

> As they swung on the turn, the sled turned over, spilling half its load.
>
> —Jack London, *The Call of the Wild* (adapted)

Note: There is more than one good arrangement for the mix. If the sentence makes sense, it is a good arrangement.

1. We brought in a few of our pals to have a little party.
   —Christy Brown, *My Left Foot*

   • while father and mother were out

   • when I was about eight

2. John Aycliffe appeared outside the cemetery walls.
   —Avi, *The Cross of Lead*

   • the **steward** [*manager*] of the **manor** [*large house*]

   • After we covered my mother's **remains** [*corpse*] with heavy earth

3. She was on the local news.
   —Sarah Dessen, *Dreamland* (adapted)

   • her eyes **blazing** [*furious*] as half the school cheered behind her

   • speaking clearly and angrily to a local reporter

4. The sailors caught an enormous shark that died on deck.
   —Isabel Allende, *Daughter of Fortune*

   • thrashing wickedly in its death **throes** [*struggle*]

   • while no one dared go near enough to club it

5. Meo stayed there in his garden.
   —Hal Borland, *When the Legends Die*

   • talking to his beans and chilies and even to himself

   • an old man with a hump on his broken back who once was a rodeo rider

ACTIVITY 3: COMBINING

Directions: Insert the **bold** parts into positions in the first sentence. Use more than one position. Underline and name each position: *opener*, *split*, *closer*.

On the Mark: Use commas to separate them from the rest of the sentence.

EXAMPLE

Amá found out I hadn't showered for five days. This happened **when I was seven.** She found out then, **so she dunked me in a scalding hot tub and scrubbed me with a brush until my skin ached.**

Combined: **When I was seven,** Amá found out I hadn't showered for five days, **so she dunked me in a scalding hot tub and scrubbed me with a brush until my skin ached.** (*OPENER, CLOSER*)

—Erika L. Sánchez, *I Am Not Your Perfect Mexican Daughter*

---

1. The ball almost hit a woman. The ball went **bouncing beyond him on the sidewalk.** The woman was **a mom with a baby carriage.**
   —Murray Heyert, "The New Kid" (adapted)

2. She looked at the family cemetery. She was **staring out the window.** The cemetery was **a small quarter-acre where barbed wire surrounded tombstones.**
   —Rebecca Skloot, *The Immortal Life of Henrietta Lacks* (adapted)

3. She would just look at you and smile. She would do something **if you asked her a question.** She would start **showing her yellow teeth.**
   —Judith Ortiz Cofer, *Silent Dancing*

4. The police entered the hotel basement. They were **holding their lanterns high**. The basement was **a cavern of brick and timber**.

—Erik Larson, *The Devil in the White City* (adapted)

5. A moth flapped in the fire of the candle. The moth was **a big one with a two-inch wingspread**. It was **dropping its abdomen into the wet wax and frazzling in a second**.

—Annie Dillard, "Death of a Moth" (adapted)

ACTIVITY 4: UNSCRAMBLING TO IMITATE

Directions: Unscramble the sentence parts to imitate the model sentence. Start with the first sentence part listed. Write out the imitation sentence and underline the mix.

On the Mark: Put commas where they appear in the model.

EXAMPLE

Model Sentence: Picturing vines reaching for him, he shuddered, their branches looping themselves around his neck. (*OPENER and CLOSER*)

—Virginia Hamilton, *M. C. Higgins, the Great* (adapted)

SENTENCE PARTS TO UNSCRAMBLE TO IMITATE THE MODEL SENTENCE:

a. (*Start here.*) Hearing the people jeering at her

b. into her thoughts

c. their criticisms inserting themselves

d. Amy cringed

Imitation Sentence: Hearing the people jeering at her, Amy cringed, their criticisms inserting themselves into her thoughts.

---

1. *Model Sentence:* His mouth open, he stopped and listened, holding his breath. (*OPENER and CLOSER*)

   —Jack Finney, "Of Missing Persons" (adapted)

   a. (*Start here.*) Her foot hurting

   b. rubbing her ankle

   c. and whimpered

   d. she sat

2. *Model Sentence:* Her husband, the banker, was a careful, shrewd man, trying hard to make her happy. (*SPLIT and CLOSER*)

   —Sherwood Anderson, *Winesburg, Ohio*

   a. (*Start here.*) The horse

   b. straining always to win the race

   c. a thoroughbred

   d. was a beautiful, fast racer

3. *Model Sentence:* Shielding his eyes from the snow, the man stopped beyond the tree and only stood there, his gloved right hand raised to his brow. (*OPENER and CLOSER*)

   —Stephen King, *Dreamcatcher*

   a. (*Start here.*) Holding her hands in her pockets

   b. and then stood still

   c. her booted cold feet protected from the ice

   d. the girl walked in the cold

4. *Model Sentence:* Looking at her husband, Mrs. Botkin, a little fat woman with white hair that lay on her forehead, started to say something. (*OPENER and SPLIT*)

    —Evan S. Connell, *Jr.*, "The Condor and the Guests" (adapted)

  a. (*Start here.*) Blinking at the sun

  b. a new lifeguard with defined muscles that showed beneath his T-shirt

  c. moved to avoid sunburn

  d. Ray Jones

5. *Model Sentence:* When the children went on a hike, she packed bird and flower guides into their **knapsacks** [*backpacks*], quizzing them on their return to see if they learned anything. (*OPENER and CLOSER*)

    —Wallace Stegner, *Crossing to Safety*

  a. (*Start here.*) While the students were in the cafeteria

  b. when she graded papers

  c. she put crayons and art paper onto their desks

  d. preparing them for the afternoon to color

ACTIVITY 5: COMBINING TO IMITATE

Directions: Combine the **bold** parts into just one sentence that imitates the model. Copy the model sentence and the imitation sentence, and in each underline the mixed tools.

On the Mark: Put commas where they appear in the model.

EXAMPLE

Model Sentence: Stu, <u>the son of a dentist who had died when Stu was seven</u>, grew up poor, <u>his father leaving his wife and two other children</u>. (*SPLIT and CLOSER*)

—Stephen King, *The Stand*

SENTENCES TO COMBINE TO IMITATE THE MODEL SENTENCE:

a. This is about the actress **Flora.**

b. She was **the star of the show who had begun acting when she was twelve.**

c. She had **started out slowly.**

d. Her starting out began with **her agent advising her appearance and specific movie roles.**

Imitation Sentence: Flora, <u>the star of the show who had begun acting when she was twelve</u>, started out slowly, <u>her agent advising her appearance and specific movie roles</u>.

---

1. *Model Sentence:* Pa, looking at the truck, squatted, his chin in his open fist. (*SPLIT and CLOSER*)

   —John Steinbeck, *The Grapes of Wrath*

a. **Willard** was there.

b. He was **looking at his child.**

c. Willard **smiled.**

d. He was hearing **his song in his happy heart.**

2. *Model Sentence:* Floating in the darkness, then the face appeared before her, a horrible face out of a nightmare. (*OPENER and CLOSER*)

   —Stephen King, *The Dead Zone*

   a. It was **playing in her mind.**

   b. Now **the dream showed** something.

   c. The dream showed **her accident.**

   d. That accident was **a terrifying incident out of her past.**

3. *Model Sentence:* His gaze locking into the distance, he would stand for hours, being hypnotized by something out there. (*OPENER and CLOSER*)

   —Michael Ondaatje, *The Cat's Table* (adapted)

   a. The pain was **his ears hurting from the gunfire.**

   b. When the pain happened, **he would run for cover.**

   c. He was **being frightened by shots.**

   d. The shots were **near there.**

4. *Model Sentence:* His small nose looking puffy and red, Charles Wallace, wearing Band-Aids on his wounds, lay on the foot of Meg's bed. (*OPENER and SPLIT*)

   —Madeleine L'Engle, *A Wrinkle in Time* (adapted)

   a. It hurt **her swollen finger.**

   b. The finger was **turning bruised and purple.**

   c. It hurt **Margaret Ann.**

   d. She was **uttering loud cries from the pain.**

   e. She **jumped around the floor of their kitchen.**

5. *Model Sentence:* The three of us in our coats and boots, we were a pitiful sight, standing among the dead stalks of winter. (*OPENER and CLOSER*)

> —Cynthia Rylant, *Missing May* (adapted)

a. There was **the cast of actors in their costumes and makeup.**

b. It seemed **they were a thrilled company.**

c. They were **bowing toward the standing audience.**

d. The ovation happened **after the play.**

ACTIVITY 6: IMITATING

Directions: Each model sentence contains a mix. Copy the model, and then find and copy its imitation. Studying those two sentences built alike, imitate the same model. Write your imitation about something you've experienced or imagined, or something you've seen on the Internet, on TV, or in a movie.

GROUP 1: MODEL SENTENCES

1. Her hands still on her hips, she chewed hard on her gum, her one foot patting the floor.

> —Rosa Guy, *The Friends*

2. The beagle, his long ears flopping, came barreling toward me, his tail sticking up like a flagpole.

> —Phyllis Reynolds Naylor, *Shiloh*

3. Sitting in a nearby leather armchair, Spencer V. Silverthorne, a young buyer for Nuget's department store, **slumbered** [*slept*].

> —Walter Lord, *A Night to Remember*

4. Slipping over the wet branches of the tree, Tim **scrambled** [*climbed fast*] downward, feeling sticky sap on his hands, hurrying.

> —Michael Crichton, *Jurassic Park* (adapted)

5. As I opened my car door, Courtney appeared, clapping, grinning, and bouncing on her tiptoes.

> —Rebecca Skloot, *The Immortal Life of Henrietta Lacks*

GROUP 1: IMITATIONS

A. The dolphin, its body surfacing, started flying over waves, its body diving down in a flash.

B. Sailing over the lush vegetation of the island, the pelican soared up, seeing other birds on the ground, eating.

C. His eyes always on the tiger, Greg backed quietly into the corner, his left hand holding the whip.

D. Hiding in a sturdy white shell, the valuable pearl, a beautiful prize for the unsuspecting ocean diver, waited.

E. When she saw the gruesome body, Janine screamed, fainting, falling, and landing on her back.

GROUP 2: MODEL SENTENCES

6. Henry, when his shaking had **subsided** [*stopped*] a little, rushed out of his cabin, leaped over the side of the boat, hurrying away down the hill through the pines.

> —John Steinbeck, *Cannery Row*

7. Standing close to the rail, Kit Tyler had been on the **forecastle** [*front*] deck since daybreak, staring hungrily at the first sight of land for five weeks.

> —Elizabeth George Speare, *The Witch of Blackbird Pond*

8. After the tyrannosaur's head crashed against the hood of the Land Cruiser and shattered the windshield, Tim was knocked flat on the seat, blinking in the darkness, his mouth warm with blood.
   —Michael Crichton, *Jurassic Park*

9. The only immigrant in my class, I was put in a special seat in the first row by the window, away from the other children, because the teacher could tutor me without disturbing them.
   —Julia Alvarez, "Snow" (adapted)

10. When the wind scarcely **swayed** [*moved*] the smoke from the oven chimney, I saw the big white clouds that darkened much later and stayed for a long time, rising slowly above the top of the bakery.
    —Pierre Gascar, "The Little Square"

GROUP 2: IMITATIONS

F. Janet, when her voice had improved a bit, sang into the microphone, harmonized with the chorus in the studio, blending seamlessly with those singers in the background.

G. As the downhill skier landed on the final stretch of the Olympic event and stopped her movement, she was absolutely in for the gold, beaming in her triumph, her eyes filling with tears.

H. When the lava slowly moved the embers from the burning bushes, he smelled the dark toxic fumes that stayed all around and poisoned for the eruption's duration, drifting everywhere around the core of the explosion.

I. An angry convict in the prison, he was held in an isolated space near the locked entrance by the hall, away from the other convicts, because the officer could watch him without upsetting others.

J. Spelling words in Helen's hands, Anne Sullivan had worked with Helen Keller for months, waiting patiently for the first sign of insight about signed language.

ACTIVITY 7: CREATING MIXES

Directions: Create a mix for the positions indicated.

EXAMPLE

Shortened Sentence: OPENER, there was an unleashed anger in his words, CLOSER.

Sample Student Mix: <u>Before he was able to control himself,</u> there was an unleashed anger in his words, <u>coming from losing the game because of his mistake.</u>

Author's Sentence: <u>When he spoke again,</u> there was an unleashed anger in his words, <u>an anger that stemmed from what he told us.</u>

—Mildred D. Taylor, *Let the Circle Be Unbroken*

1. OPENER, she was sitting on the front steps of her new house, CLOSER.

    —Sarah Dessen, *Someone Like You*

2. The car, SPLIT, jolted forward so fast that my body slammed into the black leather seat, CLOSER.

    —Stephenie Meyer, *Breaking Dawn* (adapted)

3. OPENER, I saw Margo outside my window, CLOSER.

    —John Green, *Paper Towns*

4. OPENER, the Count walked **briskly** [*quickly*] on, CLOSER.

—Amor Towles, *A Gentleman in Moscow*

5. Mrs. Hatching, SPLIT, stood looking at them proudly, CLOSER.

—Joan Aiken, "Searching for Summer"

ACTIVITY 8: BUILDING BETTER SENTENCES

The following report about Michael Phelps, Olympic gold medalist, includes some interesting information, but the writing could be stronger with tools.

GOLD

(1) He used to be an unknown. (2) It wasn't until the 2008 Olympics that he became one of the most widely recognized athletes in the world. (3) He won eight consecutive gold medals in one Olympic season.

(4) Michael Phelps had begun his career very early in his life. (5) Michael discovered that he had natural talent as a swimmer.

(6) He qualified for the Olympics at age fifteen. (7) He broke the world record for the 200-meter butterfly. (8) He entered Beijing ready to compete in the 2008 Olympics.

(9) He had no idea that he would go on to win eight gold medals.

(10) He competed victoriously in the 2012 and 2016 Olympics.

Directions: Using openers, splits, closers, and mixes, insert the tools underneath each paragraph at each caret (^). The tools are not listed in order.

GOLD

Paragraph One

(1) He used to be an unknown. (2) It wasn't until the 2008 Olympics that he became one of the most widely recognized athletes in the world, ^ . (3) He won eight consecutive gold medals in one Olympic season, ^ .

- his popularity unequaled in Olympic history

- a record that has never been equaled

Paragraph Two

(4) Michael Phelps, ^ , had begun his swimming career very early in life. (5) ^, ^, Michael, ^ , discovered that he had natural talent as a swimmer, ^ .

- setting national records for his age group

- his mind unable to stay focused in school

- a native of Baltimore, Maryland

- a ten-year-old boy diagnosed with attention-deficit disorder

- a kid super swimmer

Paragraph Three

(6) He qualified for the Olympics at age fifteen, ^ . (7) ^, he broke the world record for the 200-meter butterfly, ^ . (8) ^, he entered Beijing ready to compete in the 2008 Olympics.

- having won many gold medals in various events that included six gold medals in the 2004 Olympics

- becoming the youngest man ever to set an Olympic swimming record

- when he was age fifteen and nine months
- the youngest age for a male to qualify as an Olympic swimmer

Paragraph Four

(9) ^, he had no idea that he would go on to win eight gold medals, ^ . (10) He competed victoriously in the 2012 and 2016 Olympics, ^ , ^, ^.

- a total of twenty-three,
- the most medals that can be won by an athlete in a single season of the Olympics
- hoping to do well
- the most gold medals ever won by an Olympic athlete
- winning one gold medal after another

COMPARE: Jot down at least three reasons the version with tools is stronger than the version without tools.

QUIZ: MIXES

Directions: Jot down whether the statement is true or false.

1. A sentence with a mix contains two tools in the same position.
2. This sentence contains a mix consisting of the opener position and the split position:

    His coat wet, he stood there, holding his wet hat.

    —Ernest Hemingway, *A Farewell to Arms*

3. This sentence contains no mix:

> One morning the hobbits woke to find the large field covered with ropes and poles for tents and pavilions.
>
> —J. R. R. Tolkien, *The Fellowship of the Ring*

4. This sentence contains no mix because it uses only the closer position.

> There were two people there, a man and a woman.
>
> —Michael Crichton, *Prey*

5. A mix requires the use of two or sometimes even three different positions.

MY WRITING: SENTENCE-COMPOSING POSITIONS

Directions: Think of an interesting sports or entertainment story. Learn lots of details online about that story. Write a short report (5–10 sentences) that includes those interesting details. Like the report above about the Olympic success of Michael Phelps, use a variety of tools such as *openers, splits, closers, mixes.*

THE TOOLBOX

To get the job done right, use the right tools in the right places. You've learned all four of them: *the opener, the split, the closer, the mix.* Now get ready to use them in this section by building strong sentences. When you finish, admire your work, done right with the right tools in the right places, and take a bow!

ACTIVITY 1: PLACING ONE TOOL

Directions: Following are sentences about famous people. Add **one** of the listed tools in a good place in the sentence. Copy the sentence, underline the tool, and name its position.

On the Mark: Use a comma to separate the tool from the rest of the sentence.

1. **Amelia Earhart** became legendary as an American female pilot.

   - before she disappeared mysteriously in an attempt to fly around the world

   - the first woman pilot to fly solo across the Atlantic Ocean

   - advising flight engineers at Purdue University

   - her disappearance the subject of many best-selling books

2. **Jeff Bezos** created the world's most successful online business.

   - after he founded Amazon in his garage in 1994

   - the richest man in the world

   - marketing books in the beginning and later selling almost everything

   - his online store without a major online competitor

3. **Walt Disney** made hugely successful animated movies.

   - when he created Mickey Mouse, Donald Duck, and others

   - the holder of the record for most Academy Awards earned by an individual

   - introducing several innovations in animated cartoons

   - his animated characters among the most recognized and beloved in the world

4. **Harriet Tubman** helped to abolish slavery in the United States.

   - although she was born into slavery

   - the leader of at least thirteen missions to rescue enslaved people

   - using the Underground Railroad to help enslaved people escape

   - her protection depending on safe houses and antislavery activists

5. **Leonardo da Vinci** is best known as a famous painter.

   - although he may also have invented the parachute, helicopter, and tank

   - an individual of huge curiosity and many talents

   - having painted the famous "Mona Lisa"

   - his paintings selling for millions of dollars

ACTIVITY 2: PLACING TWO TOOLS

Directions: Add a mix of **two** of the listed tools in good places in the sentence. Copy the sentence, underline the tools, and name their positions.

On the Mark: Use commas to separate tools from the rest of the sentence.

6. **Albert Einstein** created the world's most famous equation.

   - before he received the 1921 Nobel prize in physics

- a favorite of cartoonists because of his wild hair
- creating the now famous theory of relativity
- his ideas launching entire new fields in science

7. **Marilyn Monroe** continues to be a cultural icon.

   - although she appeared in only a few movies
   - a model and an actress with a talent for comedy
   - becoming the subject of novels and nonfiction
   - her personal life plagued by failed marriages and an early death

8. **J. K. Rowling** became the world's first billionaire author.

   - although before her success she needed welfare to live
   - an example of a life that has gone from poverty to wealth
   - authoring nine novels featuring Harry Potter
   - her fantasy novels selling over 400 million copies

9. **Mahatma Gandhi** was the leader of the Indian independence movement against British rule.

   - because he believed that the British ruled India without Indian cooperation
   - a Hindu educated in law in London
   - demonstrating the power of nonviolent protest
   - his leadership and philosophy a model for Martin Luther King Jr.

ACTIVITY 3: CREATING SINGLE TOOLS

Directions: Following are sentences about famous persons. Choose any **five** sentences to create, then insert **one tool** into each sentence. Underline the tool, and name its position in parentheses: *opener*, *split*, *closer*. Before creating your tool, first learn more about the person online so your tool will be informative and interesting.

1. **Neil Armstrong** was the first person to walk on the moon.

2. **The Beatles** introduced long hair.

3. **Abraham Lincoln** delivered the famous Gettysburg Address.

4. **Nelson Mandela** went from prisoner to leader in South Africa.

5. **Elvis Presley** redefined rock and roll.

6. **Anne Frank** kept a diary during her years in hiding.

7. **Martin Luther King Jr.** championed civil rights in the United States.

8. **Alexander Hamilton** was one of the founding fathers of the United States.

9. **Barack Obama** was the first African-American president of the United States.

10. **Steve Jobs** introduced technology that people now use daily.

ACTIVITY 4: CREATING A MIX OF TWO TOOLS

Directions: Following are sentences about famous places. Choose any **five** sentences to improve, and then insert a mix of **two tools** into each sentence. Underline the tools, and name their positions in parentheses: *opener, split, closer*. Before creating your tools, learn more about the place online.

1. **The Eiffel Tower** is the most famous tourist attraction in Paris.

2. **The White House** is the official residence of the United States president.

3. **Hollywood** is the destination for many actors.

4. **The Nile River** flows through eleven countries.

5. **One World Trade Center** is also called Freedom Tower.

6. **Disneyland** is a California theme park created by Walt Disney.

7. **The Sphinx** in Egypt attracts millions of tourists.

8. **Alcatraz** is an island where a high security prison was located.

9. **Stonehenge** is a prehistoric monument in England.

10. **Graceland** is the second most visited house in the United States.

ACTIVITY 5: USING THE TOOLBOX

Directions: This is the last activity. Knock the ball out of the park for a home run. Write **five** sentences so good they could appear in a book about famous people or places. Include in each sentence a mix of two of these—*an opener, a split, a closer*. Here are some suggestions for topics.

- **FAMOUS PEOPLE**—*entertainers, athletes, inventors, heroes, explorers, authors, villains, monarchs, presidents, or other famous people*

- **FAMOUS PLACES**—*tourist attractions, cities, countries, historic sites, oddities, planets, or other famous places*

PROCEDURE

Step One: Investigate famous persons or places to find interesting information.

Step Two: Write a short sentence that begins with the name of the famous person or famous place and then makes an interesting comment about that person or place.

EXAMPLE:

Mark Zuckerberg cofounded Facebook.

Step Three: Add *a mix of two tools*.

EXAMPLES:

1. <u>Opener and Split</u>: **A computer programmer in middle school**, Mark Zuckerberg, **a world famous billionaire**, cofounded Facebook.

2. <u>Split and Closer</u>: Mark Zuckerberg, **a world famous billionaire today**, cofounded Facebook, **becoming head of the company with more than 25,000 full-time employees**.

3. <u>Opener and Closer</u>: **Working from his Harvard dormitory room**, Mark Zuckerberg cofounded Facebook, **the worldwide social media platform with billions of subscribers**.

Step Four: Repeat the process for the rest of your five sentences about famous persons, places, or some of each.

Step Five: Take a bow!

You did it! You got started with sentence composing, stayed the course, and crossed the finish line. You learned that, in building sentences, the right tool in the right place gets the job done right.

You are now a sentence architect and builder. Congratulations!

THE SENTENCE-COMPOSING APPROACH

My approach is to focus all my attention on the sentences—try to get them as good and honest and interesting as I can.

—George Saunders, *Tenth of December*
